51[%]

CHRISTIAN

51%

CHRISTIAN

Finding
Faith
AFTER
Certainty

MARK STENBERG

Fortress Press
Minneapolis

51% CHRISTIAN
Finding Faith after Certainty

Cover design: Brad Norr
Book design: PerfecType, Nashville, TN

Library of Congress Cataloging-in-Publication Data is available
Print ISBN: 978-1-5064-0019-8
eISBN: 978-1-5064-0114-1

The paper used in this publication meets the minimum requirements of American National Standard for Information Sciences — Permanence of Paper for Printed Library Materials, ANSI Z329.48-1984.

Manufactured in the U.S.A.

For Angela and Mateo, the two greatest gifts
I have ever been given.

Contents

Acknowledgments

I WOULD LIKE TO EXPRESS my deep gratitude to all of those who played a part in making this book happen. For my colleagues who challenged me and affirmed me as, together, we did this crazy job of church planting for almost twenty years: Debbie, Russell, Chris, Kyle, Kae, Wes, and Thad. For Tony and Fortress Press who are taking a chance on an unknown regional author with a shaky social media platform. (I'm so proud to be publishing a book with that "F" on the spine!) For Nadia and Joel and the kind words they included before and aft. For my amazing mom and dad, Geraldine and Arthur, and my two sisters, Shelley and Susan, who've always given me so much confidence. I'm also very grateful for the dear, sweet, brilliant, and hilarious friends I made at that curious little Christian college we attended: Pete, Jim, Marshall, Brett, Ian, Mark A., Joel, Larry, Marky C., Kyle, Scott, John S., Mark F., P.L., Dana, Doug L., Doug T-J., Doug F., Neal, and Russell. Thanks also to the very hard-working and brilliant preaching students I've had the opportunity to mentor at Luther Seminary—you make me so proud and so excited for the future of the church. And thanks most of all to the congregations of House of Mercy in St. Paul and Mercy Seat Lutheran Church in Minneapolis. It's been one of the great pleasures of my life to serve as your pastor. Thank you for sitting through some of my headier and more academic sermons—which became the stuff from which this book is made. Serving as your pastor—preaching the word and gathering around the table with you—has been one of the great treasures of my life.

Truly,

Mark Stenberg
September 2015

Foreword

A theologian of glory calls evil good and good evil. A theologian of the cross calls the thing what it actually is.

—MARTIN LUTHER, *HEIDELBERG DISPUTATION*

I CAN'T REMEMBER HOW IT was that I acquired a small "World's Greatest Christian" trophy—a Precious Moments atrocity: little girl on her knees in prayer, the ridiculous title engraved on a brass plate attached to the wooden block beneath her. But I do remember when I lost her. She was left on a windowsill in an Embassy Suites hotel room in Dallas the summer of 2009. I remember because I was devastated by the loss. She had come in remarkably handy in the two short years she was mine.

I had developed a practice, while out with friends, of placing her in front of the person who said the most Christian thing.

Mark Stenberg was the "World's Greatest Christian" more than once. I guess it took just that one extra percentage point. My own Christianity and that of our friends would so often be hovering around 45 or 50 percent, but Mark, he'd bring up Jesus, or grace, or forgiveness of sins, and *Bam!*, there she was, sitting in front of his 51 percent Christian ass once again.

My congregation, House for All Sinners & Saints, and I, their pastor, owe a lot to Mark Stenberg, along with his colleagues Debbie Blue and Russell Rathbun, with whom he founded House of Mercy, and Kae Evensen, with whom he founded Mercy Seat. These four pastors and the churches they founded are the Beatles from whom I've stolen most of my guitar riffs. They were the first people I'd ever met who dared to entertain the delusional hope that I, having met them and spent time in their churches, would also come to share: that perhaps I could serve as a parish pastor and not have to pretend to be someone else in order to do it; that scripture and Jesus could be taken seriously and this could be done without taking *ourselves* too seriously; that we could have our irony and our religion too; that the categories of liberal and conservative need not apply; and that church music didn't have to be embarrassing.

In a time when the church seems obsessed with being either relevant or purpose driven, Mark and his friends chose a third way: to be both irrelevant and purposeless. The pastoring and preaching done by my friend Mark is not meant to be self-satisfied Evangelicalism dressed up with designer jeans and light shows, nor is it a baptized version of self-improvement and corporate campaigns for personal excellence. Mark knows that when Christianity becomes a means to an end—a system through which we earn Precious Moments trophies for coolness, avoidance of suffering, personal morality, community service, or cultural standing—it has lost its true power.

There is a theological word for what happens when what we do and teach and live as Christians is an end in and of itself, and not a means to an end. That word is *freedom*. And out of freedom come healing and beauty. From freedom comes the capacity to see God in suffering and to belly-laugh in the middle of church. From freedom comes the permission to be the jagged, lovely creatures we are in the presence of a God who loves us madly.

Freedom is what I see in Mark and his work. He is unafraid to call a thing what it is. And for this I am exceedingly grateful. If only I still had that trophy, he'd get it again right about now.

Rev. Nadia Bolz-Weber
Pastor, House for All Sinners & Saints

Introduction
Getting Rid of God

What Is a Christian, and Why Should I Care?

"So you're a *Christian?*" She said it like I had just told her I was radioactive or invisible or from the galaxy Andromeda. She explained: "I went to Mass a few times as a kid. But now I'm a Buddhist. It's just so less judgmental. It's a better fit for me."

"I can definitely understand the appeal," I confessed, "what with the crazy, violent, and competitive world we live in. What a gift it is to be able to detach and let go of this false self that craves attention and these empty possessions at which we clutch and grab."

She smiled and nodded, relieved that I wasn't a fundamentalist kook who was going to pester her about Jesus. And then she turned the conversation back toward me: "What does it mean to be a Christian?"

We were in row 20, seats D and E of a Boeing 737 on a nonstop flight to San Francisco, just settling in and buckling up. She had noticed the book I was reading, *God for Us*, spelled out in

1

giant silver letters on the spine.[1] I wondered whether this would be a three-hour conversation or just a polite, passing exchange.

Am I a Christian?, I asked myself. To be honest, a lot of the time I don't feel like it. And when I read the actual stories of Jesus, I seriously wonder if I am worthy of the name. But I didn't know what else to say. So I simply said, "Yes, I'm an agnostic about a lot of things, but I do believe that God is sheer unconditional grace, and I believe that God has been revealed to the world in the life, death, and resurrection of Jesus, who we humbly call 'the Christ.'"

She stared at me with a blank expression. I could tell that even those words were far too churchy, too in-house Christian-speak. That's a problem for those of us on the inside. We lose touch with how culturally meaningless these words have become.

God Is Dead, Long Live Relationship

Take the word *God*, for instance. This word is dead. Through sheer overuse, it has been emptied of meaning. Our popular notions of God include:

- God of the politicians, invoked to win the hearts and minds of voters
- God "the man in the sky" to whom athletes point when they make a play
- God who shames us into better behavior
- God who condemns most of the world's population to hell
- God the answerer of desperate prayers
- God as an idea that we think our way to
- God the first cause, who wound it all up and let it go
- God the exclamation (OMG!)

---

1. A breathtakingly gorgeous book by the late great Catherine LaCugna, a feminist theologian who taught at Notre Dame and died of cancer in 1997. *God for Us: The Trinity and Christian Life* (San Francisco: Harper Collins, 1992.)

None of these vague and general notions of God come anywhere near to capturing God incarnate, God *for us*, God made flesh in the suffering servant of Jesus of Nazareth, who died a horrifying and gruesome death at the hands of the extremely violent and barbaric Roman Empire.

What we need is to completely reboot, recover, reconstruct our notion of God. I propose that we substitute the word *God* with *relationship*. Thus, if I could return to that conversation with that passing stranger on the plane, I would say something like this: "I don't believe in God so much as I believe in relationship. Rather I trust that the experience of relationship itself—the intense, uncanny, risky, but loving bond that can exist between creatures—is the highest high, the truest truth we can know—relationship like that deep, primal connection that exists between a mother and a child. The question is, where does relationship come from? My answer is that it emanates from a God of pure, self-giving love, revealed to us in Jesus the Christ and made real to us by the Holy Spirit of God's suffering love."

Relationship as a Lens

Being done with God and venturing into this new terrain of relationship, what would it look like to examine Christian faith through this new lens? That's the purpose of this book. (Spoiler alert.) I take the classic topics of the faith and view them through the lens of the loving relationship of grace. Revelation, the Trinity, God, Jesus, the atonement, the Holy Spirit, the created world, sin, heaven, hell, the church—what do these subjects look like when viewed through the lens of the self-sacrificial, relational, love of Father, Son, and Spirit?

As such, this is a book about theology, an arena that can be boring, academic, dry, dangerous, but at best wonderfully bliss-ful. At its worst, theology has been in service to all manner of barbarism and torture, invoking the divine to justify the most

heinous forms of violence. But theology is also capable of breath-
taking beauty. What if you could hear words that made you feel
profoundly hopeful, words that made you feel deeply and unconditionally loved, words that assured you that grace, forgiveness,
and hope for all of creation are not just the sentimental whims of
a few deluded dreamers but concrete historical realities? That is
what theology is capable of. Or to be more precise, it's the subject
matter that theology is called to reflect upon.[2]

What is theology?, you might be asking. There are a zillion
ways to define it. I take it to mean something like this: theology
is a second-order critique of the first-order event of the Word
of God. The first order stuff is primary, central, the core, the
raw, in-your-face encounter with the divine. Though they differ
on the details, Christians believe that God shows up, that revelation happens, through scripture, preached word, sacrament,
prayer, imagination, silent meditation, the created world, and
other means. Christians display a wide variety of understandings as to *how* God is revealed, but they do believe in some sort
of self-revelation of God as the source of their faith. Think of
this first order experience as the primary stuff of the divine
encounter.[3]

The practice of theological reflection, or "theology" for
short—which is what I am attempting in the bulk of this book—
is the gift of stepping back from that first order encounter and
asking questions. If God speaks, how do we best understand? If
there is a Word from God, what does it mean for humanity and
for all of creation? How are we to behave? How do we be open to

---

2. Not that there's no bad news. We'll learn all about the bad news in chapter
10. But for now, just know this: the bad news is properly understood only in the
light of the good news, the knowledge that it will be overcome.

3. In classic reformation based Protestantism (my tradition) this first order
event is called "proclamation," the preached word of the love of God revealed in
the life, teachings, and works of the risen and crucified Christ interpreted and
acted out in the sacrament of holy communion.

hearing that word again? How do we think critically about the ways in which this divine revelation has been distorted? Understood this way, the woman's question to me on the plane was theology, my response to her was theology, and the ways I've continued to wrestle with her question and wish I'd answered it differently are theology.

All stripped down, theology is the *gift* of stepping back from the worship and proclamation of the church and asking the big questions: Where is the good news? How do we best proclaim it? And how in the devil has the church managed to turn the good news into bad news? Sometimes that happens in seminary classrooms, sometimes in row 20 of a flight from MSP to SFO.

51 Percent Christian?

Oh, and a word about the title of this book. How can you be 51 percent Christian? That's ridiculous! Of course it is. It's supposed to be. Can you measure your faith in percentage points? No, but I'm trying to get at something more serious. We've somehow come to believe that faith is all or nothing, that you're either a 100 percent Christian or not a Christian at all. That puts way too much pressure on us. Faith becomes a series of mental exercises in which your little brain attempts to triumph over whatever source of doubt might arise. Not only does that run counter to what the Bible says, it is also hopelessly self-centered, not to mention exhausting.

In confessing that I am a 51 percent Christian, I'm trying to tell you that you have permission to doubt, to question, to stand on a barren heath on the coast of Denmark and shake your tiny fist in anger at God. But in the end, it's not about you. Faith is about relationship, and that is the only way it makes even a lick of sense. What if this God we profess faith in is, essentially, *relationship?* Then faith in God becomes something that you choose every day. Or better yet, it chooses you.

After Certainty

In two thousand years of Christian history, we've witnessed countless episodes in which the certainty of the faithful has legitimized discrimination, persecution, violence, and war. During such dark times, certainty has become an idol, with truly tragic results. Humans created God in the image of their culture, their clan, or their tribe, and then they extracted from their idol-god some indisputable "will of God" that somehow perfectly corresponded with their arrogance, exclusion, and condemnation.

In my tongue-in-cheek embrace of this "51 percent Christian" moniker, I'm actually getting at something very serious. *Certainty just might be the enemy of faith.* Though I'd be glad to take credit for that intuition, it's really nothing new. In trying to knock down the idol of certainty, I'm following in the tradition of two of Christendom's more imaginative thinkers: Blaise Pascal, a Frenchman who lived in the mid-1600s, and nineteenth-century Danish philosopher Søren Kierkegaard. They are the two great critics of dogmatic certainty. Instead of appealing to foundational, rigid, preestablished truths, Pascal and Kierkegaard reveled in tension, irony, inversion, satire, story, and surprise. They trusted in a living word that is always new and can never be captured in the certainty of a system.

We are, after all, living in a postcertain world. As we continue to wrestle with and criticize the modern era, the quest for grand foundational truths is crumbling. Academic disciplines are becoming more limited and humble about the scope of their respective knowledge. Even in the sciences, researchers and scholars are recognizing limits and paradigm shifts. Isn't it time that Christians embrace this postcertain climate we now inhabit and open ourselves to more honest and fruitful dialogue with all sorts of academic practices and disciplines?

Finally, what about that movement that, at present, is growing much faster than Christianity: namely, atheism? Must Christians be always at war with atheists? What if there is another way? Instead of fear and exclusion and argument, what if we could be more open to engaging our atheist sisters and brothers in meaningful action and reflection about the state of our world? Bertrand Russell, forefather to the likes of Richard Dawkins, Christopher Hitchens, and Daniel Dennet, has an oft-quoted quip that gets to the heart of the danger of certainty: "The fundamental cause of the trouble is that in the modern world the stupid are cocksure while the intelligent are full of doubt."[4] Brother Bertrand hints at the possibility of a climate in which *both* Christians and atheists are a bit less certain of their claims and much more open to common action and reflection on matters of peace, justice, ethics, and environmental action.[5]

Operating Instructions

According to some recent surveys, more than half of current readers fail to read books to their completion. But here's good news about this book. *You do not have to read the whole thing!* And you do not have to read it in order. This book will be a topical journey through the teachings of the faith. The chapters surely are related to each other, but you are welcome to pick and choose as you go.

I write because I have this desire to point, and I can't make it go away.

There is a set of paintings on display at the Unterlinden Museum in France. They are huge and haunting, and the colors are spectacular: oil paints so thick and textured you can almost smell them. Matthias Grünewald's Isenheim Altarpiece was first

---

4. Bertrand Russell, *Mortals and Others*, vol. 2, *Bertrand Russell's American Essays, 1931–1935* (London: Routledge, 1998), 28.

5. I must give credit to my brilliant friend Christopher Zumski-Finke for helping me come up with this title. We hope to collaborate on a jointly authored follow-up to this book: *The New Pragmatism: A 51% Christian and an Uncertain Atheist Discuss God, Ethics, Parenting, and the Environment.*

installed on the altar at the Monastery of Saint Anthony in Isenheim. At the time, the monastery served as a hospital, a place
of care for victims of the black plague and other skin diseases,
where the noble monks of Antonine risked their lives to care
for the dying and the dead. The central panel of the altarpiece
features a dying Christ on the cross. His remarkably muscular
body is covered in pockmarks and sores. To the right of the cross
is an anachronism. John the Baptist is standing there. Anyone
with even a remedial knowledge of the four Gospels in the Bible
knows that John the Baptist was long gone by the time of Jesus'
crucifixion. And yet, here is John.

Although the figure of Jesus is front and center, many observ-
ers are struck by a second image. John is pointing. His elongated,
bony, fleshy finger is straining to point at the corpse on the cross.
John's finger is speaking the message "Look, here is God. God
is present in our affliction. In fact, God is for us in such a deep,
intimate, painfully passionate way that God became this. This is
the picture of love."

All I want out of life is to be the fleshy, bony, elongated index
finger in that Grünewald altarpiece. John the Baptist, pointing,
pointing to the crucified Christ, the one who calls us to die, that
we might be born again. As I seek to point to this love that comes
from beyond, from outside, from the heart of God, my hope is
that, as you learn what it is to which I point, you will be inspired
to do your own pointing. You, in your own peculiar way.

1

How the Cheatin' Heart of Modernity Double-Crossed the Doctrine of Revelation

THE THING ABOUT US is that we like information. We like it a lot—more so than probably any other culture that has ever existed on the face of the earth. This is both a blessing and a curse. Information can be a good thing. I am grateful for the right information whenever my cell phone works, or I take off on an airplane, or I listen to the song I just downloaded on my iPod, Louis Armstrong's "What a Wonderful World." In other words, information is good and useful as an *instrument.* But is information enough?

As people who are bounded by modernity, we've grown up with this optimism. We can trust our brains, right? If only we have the right information, the right inputs, we can fix things, like MacGyver. The knowability and fixability of all things has become our religion.

Instrumental Reason, an American Idol

But can information *save* us? With our information in hand, we can attempt to set a proper course, to fix our bearings, to head in the right direction. But you know what? The human heart is prone to outsmarting our information in some pretty damn devious ways. We can take good information and manipulate it.[1] We can ignore some of the information, bend other parts of it, and completely overemphasize those bits that set us in the best possible light. We do all that in ways that mask our self-deception, our violence, our greed, and our apathy about each other and about the world. In other words, information is good and useful as an *instrument*. But can mere information kick our butt and confront us and expose to us the myriad delusions and self-deceptions of which we are capable?[2]

Regarding the task of theology, our overconfidence in information has some downright radioactive fallout. First of all, we are prone to the overbelief that *all* knowledge is propositional: that

---

1. Yes, as a matter of fact, this is a thinly veiled reference to President George W. Bush and his cronies (Cheney, Wolfowitz, Rove, and Rumsfeld) and their "we know better than you" manipulation of the data that sucked us into the quagmire that is Iraq. But this issue is way bigger than our politics. We all do this, you know. When I point a finger at you, there are four fingers pointing back at me. Well, not really, because my thumb is pointing up in the air. But you know what I mean, right?

2. Any philosopher worth her or his salt will at one time or another wrestle with the question of self-critique. From whence comes self-critique? In other words, can anyone, anywhere, anyhow ever simply stand up and tell us to our face that we are full of crap? Especially when the weight of traditions and institutions blur and squash and crazify voices that claim that something is wrong? The best of the Christian tradition trusts that there is such a thing as the event of the Word of God, a Word that judges us and forgives us at the same time, a Word that completely levels us and helps us hear the ugly truth about ourselves only because we are first told that we are unconditionally loved and completely forgiven. It's a truth that allows vision and insight and death-and-rebirth, and it sets us free to actually do what is right, for the right reasons. But more on that in our chapter on ethics.

everything worth knowing can be reduced to true or false statements that could be set down in writing on some grand cosmic blackboard of truth. Second of all, like a bad mime trapped in an invisible bubble, we get stuck inside these paradigms whose walls we don't even see. Third of all, our overconfidence in information has stymied our imagination. What if truth could be an *event*—an event that happens to us and takes us to some new place, some place that we hitherto were not even capable of imagining?

So it's time for one of those pithy, grandiose, manifesto-esque declarations, this one regarding the oft-misunderstood doctrine of revelation. Here you go. (Make a power fist and thrust it in the air as you shout this out loud—I dare you.)

Modernity has stolen our doctrine of revelation!
It's time for us to steal it back!

What if information is not enough? What if we are more lost than that? What if we are not just wrong or in error or missing the right inputs? What if the human heart is much more devious than that? What if revelation is not about information? What if it is all about something I will call *the incongruity of grace?*

Go to College, Lose Your Faith (a Personal Narrative Told in the Second Person so It Doesn't Sound Quite So Self-Indulgent)

So. You go to college, you lose your faith.

You know the script. Its starts in your sociology class—this notion that religion is, in reality, nothing more than a social force that binds people together, a human construction to fend off the chaos of our fleeting, fragile existence. You hear the same thing in your philosophy class. And your psychology class. Before you know it, even your badminton class fails to proclaim the glory of God. Especially when you get beat by everyone in the whole class. (I'm speaking hypothetically here, people.)

Of course. It all makes perfect sense. You now have some new *information*. You have been enlightened. And it all is quite reasonable: Religion is a sort of social force. Like Santa Claus, religion sees you when you're sleeping and knows when you're awake. So you better not pout or cry or lie or cheat or fail to renew your license tabs, or things might just fall apart.

And of course, in your newly enlightened, more rational state, you recognize that religion is also extremely dangerous—the opiate of the masses, the anesthetic that numbs people's minds and keeps them in their place. As an idealistic young college student, you find yourself reading Karl Marx *and loving it.* In fact, you deeply *feeeeel* the elegant yet heavy words of his eleventh thesis on Feuerbach: "The philosophers have only interpreted the world, in various ways; the point is to change it."[3]

So. You become a post-Christian little zealot. You're still trying to change the world, only this time for the sake of justice instead of Jesus. You end up being extremely critical of almost everyone, except a select few, your friends, who are pretty much just like you.

Revelation Part Three: Mrs. Turpin Gets Hit with the Book

But what if *revelation* has nothing to do with information, nothing to do with the correct knowledge of God? What if it has nothing to do with *religion?* What if revelation is something we can't do? What if it's not something we can think or behave or believe ourselves into? What if it's something that *happens* to us, like Mrs. Turpin getting hit with the book?

Ruby Turpin, the protagonist in a Flannery O'Connor short story, is a large, cheerful white woman from the south who is obsessed with ranking people. She goes about "singing gospel songs in her head" and praising Jesus, the same Jesus who "spared

---

3. Frederick Engles, *Ludwig Feuerbach and the End of Classical German Philosophy* (Peking: Foreign Language Press, 1976), 65.

her from being born white trash," and gave her a "cheerful dispo-sition" and "a little of everything." All the while, she's distracted by her own personal Jesus from seeing how profoundly racist, judgmental, and self-obsessed she really is.[4]

Then one day she goes to town to see the doctor, because her husband, Claude, has been kicked in the leg by a cow. She is wait-ing in the doctor's office, mentally sorting out and judging and ranking all the people in the small waiting room, and humming a gospel song to herself. And she gets hit, with a book, right between the eyes, and knocked unconscious. The book is thrown by a character named Mary Grace. The book? It is a large, hard-bound textbook entitled *Human Development*. The title of the short story? "Revelation."

Now, it's really no fun to explain a great story, so I'll just say this: What if revelation is always, in some way, something that flies across the room and conks us on the head? Something unexpected, un-self-initiated, and bewildering. What if, for some reason, it *must* come to us from out of the blue, as if it's something we cannot simply tell ourselves?

And thus we arrive at the center of our subject matter: the incongruity of grace. The *incongruity of grace* means this: that grace does not fit the expected pattern, that it always comes to us, not from within, but from outside; that it is always a terrible but blessed interruption of our same old same old story of envy, jealousy, isolation, self-justification, and greed.

If religion is an attempt to control and behave, revelation is more like an interruption, a rift, a fissure. If the religious person wants to go up, to ascend, to climb up to God, the God of the Bible is a God who comes down. If this is so, then religion must control and bind. But revelation must *shatter*.[5]

---

4. Flannery O'Connor, "Revelation," in *Everything That Rises Must Converge* (New York: Farrar, Straus and Giroux, 1965), 508.
5. Jacques Ellul, *Living Faith: Belief and Doubt in a Perilous World* (New York: Harper and Row, 1983), 110–21.

Why? Why would God come and disturb us—hit us with the book, right between the eyes? Well, quite simply, God is *for us.* For us in ways we can't expect and anticipate. And because we have this ancient proclivity for making God in our own image, for thinking of God as a great big one of us, the revealing grace of God casts its judgment upon our violent and destructive idols and hits us right between the eyes.

What if revelation *is* more like getting hit with a book than receiving information or moral instruction? How would you communicate that? For all its downright explosive potential, the church has been wildly unimaginative in proclaiming this radical grace. Word to the preacher people (you know who you are): *please,* starting now, write sermons that are shocking, puzzling, morbid, twisted, disturbing, fleshy, messy, and beautiful. We've been given this great gift of proclamation. Why are we so timid? Why are we being so religious? Why are we merely giving how-to lessons on successful living when we are called to preach this Word that cuts people open and makes them bleed?[6]

Revelation brings with it its own kind of uncertainty and ambiguity. No longer can we build a system. No longer can we try to control things. A radical openness has been born. The question is not, "Will I have faith tomorrow?" but rather, "What will I make of this revelation tomorrow? How will I come to renew my understanding of it?"[7] Or, perhaps, more accurately, How will God reveal Godself, and what will I make of it?

A Frenchman once told me that "the really unbearable thing for us is grace."[8] Grace disturbs us, throws us off balance, exposes our cultural morality, and puts us in front of a mirror. But grace also liberates us.

---

6. I am so proud of the brilliant and hard-working preaching students I've had the opportunity to mentor. You know who you are. Thank you for your hard work and your creativity. Memo to the rest of the church: let's create kind, generous, adventurous, and affirming environments in which these voices will renew and reform the church.

7. Ibid., 120.

8. Ibid., 117.

Deconceptualizing the Bible

The Bible is not a collection of propositions about God. At their best, Christians understand the Bible as a *living word* that has the power to disturb, provoke, shock us into seeing. The Bible is a living record of God's dealing with humans in sneaky, subversive ways—taking up residence here, in our midst, slowly, achingly, bleedingly, seeking to overcome our arrogance, our violence, our hubris. The Bible is the record of God teasing us, luring us ahead, tricking us into seeing things as they are. Because we need so much more than information. We need for the out to become the in, the down to become the up, a little child to lead us.

Take the story of David and Nathan. David was a great king. Some consider him to be the greatest king of all. Well, as the story goes, during that time of the year "when kings march forth," David just happened to stay behind in Jerusalem. One evening, he got up from his couch and "walked around on the roof of the palace" (2 Samuel 11:2, NIV). He looked down from his roof and saw a young woman, Bathsheba, bathing. She was beautiful—her hair, her smooth, olive-toned skin, her long limbs. And he was filled with desire for her. He *had* to have her. So he justified it to himself, made the numbers add up. He looked at the information and constructed this reality: "She is the most beautiful woman I have ever seen, and I am the king," and so on and so forth. And in the name of his desire, he dreamed up an elaborate plan to have her husband killed in battle, by David's own enemies. Chillingly devious. *The Godfather* times ten. Yes, he talked himself into it.

Then what happened? Nathan, his best friend, Nathan, the prophet, told him a little story.[9] (And I paraphrase.)

---

9. As found in 2 Samuel 12:1-6. In Hebrew tradition, kings were supposed to govern in conjunction with the priests and prophets. But rarely did the kings listen. It seems the executive power went to their heads. Hmmmm.

There were two men in a certain city, the one rich and the other poor. The rich man had everything. The poor man had nothing, except for one little lamb, which he adored. He—and his children—loved their little lamb. They raised it and played with it and fed it from their table. The poor man even used to cradle it in his arms, like he did with his own little girl.

But then the rich man in the city was about to do some entertaining. And wanting to impress his visitors, he decided to throw them a feast. So he took the little lamb that belonged to the poor man, and he slaughtered it and fed it to his guests at the party.

When David heard this little story, he was outraged: "The man who has done this deserves to die!" And no sooner did those words leap from his mouth than he looked into the eyes of his best friend, Nathan, and got hit with the Word. The truth was revealed. "I am the man. I am the man in that story. And I deserve to die."

Revelation is not simply knowledge or information or statements or propositions. Revelation confronts us, shakes us up, rattles our bones, shows us the ugly truth about us.

God confronts us, in shocking, grotesque, surprising, unexpected ways. Why? Because God is *for us*, in ways we can't even imagine. Because God will not leave us alone. Because God takes up residence here, right smack dab in our violence, our lust, our greed, our self-centeredness, and our self-loathing. And God's love is right here, in our midst, working to lead us back home.

The Resurrection as the Extreme Incongruity of Grace

So there's this professor of theology, James Alison. He's got the dope, and I'm addicted. Or to state this in a more professional way, I am confident that Alison's is a compelling way of telling the Jesus story in our context (which is about all a poor theologian can hope for).

According to Alison, the story of Jesus and his cross tells us, in graphic detail, how we lynched an innocent victim. We all participated—some by leading, others by following.[10]

We are told that it was envy that led to Jesus' death. He fulfilled a prophecy that he would be hated without cause, that he would be counted among sinners, unjustly. The logic of his executioners is right there, in the text of John: "It is better to have one man die for the people than to have the whole nation destroyed."[11]

But after this lynching, a strange thing happened. It came to be understood how Jesus taught his disciples to leave behind the old world of violence, how to take the side of the excluded, those who are victimized, all the victims of history. But just *how* did this happen? What happened, that they could somehow understand the innocence of the victim and the gravity of their violence? What happened, that the disciples began to change the world, really to take the side of the victim and resist the violence of the empire?[12]

Something happened that made Jesus not just one more dead man, crushed by the violence. That something that happened was the *resurrection*. The resurrection is the source and center of all incongruities of grace; this utterly grace-filled incongruity of an innocent victim returning from the dead, who loves us, and forgives us, and holds up a mirror to our violence.

The resurrection is not an idea. And thus Christian revelation can never be a theory or a concept. Rather, the resurrection

---

10. Ought a white, North American theologian be permitted to use the language of lynching? Given the history of slavery and oppression in the Americas, for some the term *lynching* has much more visceral and, yes, painful overtones. I use this term only in great deference and respect, in the spirit of the even more personal and powerful analysis of Jesus as the victim of a mob lynching found in James Cone's *The Cross and the Lynching Tree* (Maryknoll, NY: Orbis, 2013).

11. James Alison, *Raising Abel: The Recovery of the Eschatological Imagination* (New York: Crossroad, 1996), 1–13.

12. Ibid.

is an event, something that happened in time, in history, to a certain group of people, who then began to tell others about it.

We are mired in the violence. But God, by diving into creation in this crucified and risen victim, turns our violent story upside down and inside out. In this utterly subversive action, God turns those of us who are rivals into friends. And now we have permission to creatively admire and imitate and encourage each other, and to help each other take the side of the victim, all the victims of history.

This is revelation, and welcome to it. This is the incongruity of grace—that God took our story of a violent lynching and through the resurrection of the victim turned it into a peaceful un-lynching that now floods the world with hope.

Conclusion: Revelation You Can Eat and Drink

Up to this point, our journey through revelation has been rather dark and brooding: Flannery O'Connor, King David, and all this violence and self-deception and rivalry. Well, have I got a happy ending for you. Actually, it's not my own. I stole it from the writer of the third gospel, Luke.

Near the end of his gospel, Luke tells one of the great practical jokes in all of literature. It's been called "The Road to Emmaus." Here's Jesus, freshly risen from the dead. He's walking along with two strangers. And he *doesn't tell them who he is!* It takes them a long, long time to get the reveal, the *revelation*. In fact, they don't even begin to understand it until much later, when he sits down at the table with them and they pass around the bread and the wine.

According to Luke, the thing that opened their eyes and made him known to them was the breaking of the bread (Luke 24:1-35, NRSV). He fed them. And here's where these words on this page dissolve away, and you put yourself at the table—with me and all the strange and wonderful and broken and wounded people all over the world who gather at this table.

For in the end, according to Luke's gospel, Jesus is "made known to them in the breaking of the bread" (Luke 24:25, NRSV). In fact, according to some hard-core sacramentalists in the church, revelation is not at all something we assent to or believe or feel. It's something that happens, perpetually and ontologically. Christ is revealed, made present to us in the holy Mass, the Eucharist, this meal. No matter what we, at the moment, might feel or think or believe, we are united with Christ and with each other in this meal. It is revelation that we eat and drink.

And this is the part where my words fail. I'm sorry, but try as I might, I just can't serve you Communion through this book. Nor have my attempts at Virtual Eucharist been successful. No, in order to receive *this* revelation, you are going to have to drop your dignity, swallow your pride, and go to church. Oh, I know, going to church won't be easy. It's inconvenient and messy, and you'll have to put up with all these ridiculous, fleshy, feuding humans with their quirks and key rattling at the wrong time and their epic mood swings between grandiosity and self-loathing. But, hey, the church is still your best bet if you want to hear the proclamation of God's incongruous grace and actually chew and swallow this revelation that was initiated by Jesus himself. Besides, the Apostle Paul commanded it. He said, "For as often as you eat this bread and drink the cup, you proclaim the Lord's death until he comes" (1 Corinthians 11:26, NRSV). What could be better than that? And all the words I could ever hope to write about revelation are a mere shadow of what happens in this meal, at which the risen victim pronounces our judgment and our forgiveness and sentences us to life with each other.

2

Death to the Conceptual Trinity! An Anti-Monotheistic Manifesto

WELCOME TO OUR TRINITY chapter. This chapter will unfold like a play in three acts. Our first act will identify an error the contemporary church has fallen into, namely forcing an event of history into explanatory models (analogies) that obscure the passionate intensity of the greatest love story every told. Act two will trace the history of three monotheisms of modernity that, again, obscure the deep intimate passion of the story by making it all about a great big giant god who is the master, the *Grand Divine Subject*, the controller of all things. Finally, in act three, the author will humbly offer up a resolution rooted in relationship—imaging the divine as a relational reality rooted in history, time, flesh, mud, blood, and bone—this mad passionate love that has entered creation and is luring it toward completion.

Act One: Food for Thought—Our Fall from Event to Concept

A story about our fall, which begins with an apple.

A Sunday school teacher is trying to teach children about the doctrine of the Trinity. She is holding an apple. She slices it open. She proceeds to tell the children about the skin of the apple, the flesh of the apple, and the seeds, and about their conceptual counterparts, the Father, the Son, and the Holy Ghost. Three in one. One in Three. Skin, flesh, seeds . . . Father, Son, Spirit. Three in one. One in three.

The children look puzzled. They don't understand. They *want* to know about God (even though they've been led to believe that Jesus is *nicer* than God). But they just shrug their shoulders and say to themselves, "Well, I guess this is just something I won't be able to understand until I grow up."

Little do they know that when it comes to the Trinity, adults don't have a clue either. And the greatest irony of all? Our analogies, like the apple, actually confuse and complicate the matter instead of bringing clarity. To the degree that our analogies are conceptual and not historical, they remove us from the realm of creation, history, and time, and they place the Trinity in the realm of ideas instead of events.

Meanwhile, in that same Sunday school classroom, there's a print, a crucifixion scene of Jesus, hanging on the wall. If Jesus could speak, he'd be shouting, "Hey, teacher! Over here! Get rid of that silly apple, and just look at what *happened*. It's way simpler than you're making it out to be. Just tell them that God the Father is *here*, in the event of the cross, and our Spirit of this act of love is working in creation to overcome all that is opposed to it."

Act Two: Our Backslidden Condition—Two Modern Variations of Monotheism and One That's Been Born Again

Because of this same sort of overconceptualized, theory-laden talk about the Trinity, modernity's brazen razor of instrumental reason grabbed the Trinity by whatever you grab a Trinity by and sheared off two-thirds of it. In other words, because we've been tempted to treat the Trinity as an idea in our minds rather than an event in history, the church has veered off into these monotheisms that are not about the event of the crucified Christ and the relationship of Father, Son, and Spirit. This has been pointed out, with great precision, in an article written by Gary Simpson, a theologian who teaches at Luther Seminary. According to Simpson, modernity has bequeathed us two forms of monotheism, one "moral" and the other one "experiential."[1]

1. Moral Monotheism

Handed down from Immanuel Kant (1724–1804), moral monotheism reduces religion to morality, casting aside the Trinity as a bit of ancient superstition without practical relevance. Moral monotheism proclaims a Jesus as archetype, a moral mentor for the conduct of reasonable persons. In other words, Kant wanted to strip away the superstitious and hard-to-swallow details of the Christian story and get down to what it is really about: *being good.* That hard-to-swallow stuff about the death and resurrection of Jesus is glossed over with this new and improved universal morality that everyone can get with. So without even realizing it, modernity left us with this "moral law within" that we think is

---

1. Gary Simpson, "No Trinity, No Mission: The Apostolic Difference of Revisioning the Trinity," *Word and World* 18, no. 3 (Summer 1998): 264–71.

some sort of universal truth but is actually part of the historical tradition of modernism.

It's right there in the fabric of our culture, in all these pop-culture notions of conscience and do-goodism. Yes, moral monotheism is still alive in all these cultural trappings that appeal to some mysterious but universal "moral law within," such as Walt Disney's *Pinocchio* ("Always let your conscience be your guide"), certain gosh-why-aren't-they-smarter members of the Supreme Court who make decisions based on "natural law," and episodes of *The Brady Bunch* or *That's So Raven* that treat the ethical dilemmas of adolescent girls.

Morality without the cross. It's a tidy, once-born monotheism in which we identify God with our conscience instead of a twice-born death and resurrection, which costs much more, is way messier, and demands much more of us—our very lives.

2. Experiential Monotheism

The monotheism of direct religious experience also is still very much woven into the fabric of our modern tradition. Here we avoid that messy cross stuff, the event that manifests the Trinity, by a more direct appeal to "religious experience" or "intuition" or "feeling." In our day, this "religious experience," this direct encounter with the divine has become something of a commodity, traded in books and seminars and websites.

Friedrich Schleiermacher (1768–1834) was one of the pioneers of this tradition. Schleiermacher found himself caught between the simple Christian faith and practice he learned in his home and his newfound appreciation for philosophy, rationalism, art, science, and culture he discovered in the big cities of Halle and Berlin. His attempt to resolve these two conflicting sets of influences manifested itself in a historic publication, *On Religion: Speeches to Its Cultured Despisers*, in which Schleiermacher tried to convince his cultured peers that religion ought to be valued and respected as a science.

In the name of trying to defend the Christian faith, Schlei-ermacher proposed that "religious feeling" is not backwoods and infantile but rather the most sublime and lofty reality of which humans are capable. Schleiermacher's "religious experience" appealed to a deep and abiding "sense and taste for the Infinite" through an "intuition of the Infinite in the finite." Here, Jesus is held up as a fully realized human being distinguished by the "constant potency of his God-consciousness."[2]

Even if you appreciate this "constant potency" (and who wouldn't?), the *critics* of modernity—Nietzsche, Freud, and Marx—seem like they'd be way more fun to hang out with at a barbeque. I mean, who cares about religion as religion? A sense and taste for the infinite in the finite? What *is* that? It sounds more like a really good meal at my favorite French restaurant than anything to do with a homeless Palestinian Jew who asks his followers to die.

Experiential monotheism calls upon a modern Jesus to awaken religious experience. But all the stuff that is wrong with experiential monotheism bids me to lay down a string o' ques-tions. In the contemporary marketplace of religion, in which I can choose whatever religion seems the most fashionable, convenient, and appealing, what does it matter that it is *Jesus* who brings this awakening? And what does the event of the cross matter if we can simply "look within" to locate our God-consciousness? And how will we know when we find it? Is it kind of like finding your car keys?

Not to mention, this is all fine and good while sitting in the comfort of your Barcalounger, but what about the very real experience of human suffering? Can "religious experience" really provide any comfort, hope, or promise in the depth of violence, despair, grief, exploitation, or environmental destruction?

---

2. Friedrich Schleiermacher, *On Religion: Speeches to Its Cultured Despisers*, trans. J. Oman (New York: Harper & Row, 1958), 36–45.

3. Evangelical Monotheism

The Evangelicals have attempted to offer a living and vital alternative to moral and experiential monotheisms. But at its worst, the story the Evangelicals tell is monotheistic as well. Placing too much emphasis on a substitutionary view of atonement, Evangelicals are prone to pitting God the Father against Jesus the Son. In a slightly caricatured telling (but only slightly), Evangelicals proclaim the following story: Humans are really, really naughty. In fact, they are tainted by original sin. This elicits the wrath of a righteous God, whose justice is besmirched. The cross is the place of punishment. Jesus takes a beating so that his little brothers and sisters can get off the hook with their angry father.

The story is easily told and easily passed on. But is it faithful to the Trinitarian event of the cross in which God the Father is *present*? Fortunately, this violent story impinges upon only a few areas of the Evangelical understanding of Scripture. It appears to be limited to (1) their understanding of the Hebrew Bible, (2) their interpretation of the New Testament epistles, and (3) their understanding of the Gospels. Of course, many Catholics, Lutherans, and even the unaffiliated tote around this image of the meaning of the cross. Who wouldn't want to reject that God? (Please see chapter 6 for a more in-depth discussion of the meaning of atonement.)

Act Three: The Recovery of the Trinity—a Good Excuse to Say the Name "Zizioulas"

In the face of these well-intentioned but distorted monotheisms, the church is called to recover the proclamation of the *event* of the Trinity. The Trinity is neither a concept nor a theory. Rather, it is bound to the old, old story of the cross of Christ. Its leading affirmation is that God is there, in the event of the cross. By proclaiming the presence of God the Father in the event of the cross, the church counters the speculation and abstraction of conceptual thinking about the Trinity. As put by Jürgen Moltmann, the doctrine of the Trinity stems from "the event of Golgotha, the event of the love of the Son and the grief of the Father from which the Spirit who opens up the future and creates life, in fact derives." In other words, "the place of the doctrine of the Trinity is not the 'thinking of thought,' but the cross of Jesus."[3] According to Catherine LaCugna, proclaiming the event of the Trinity in the cross, the church sets forth the message that God is "essentially relational, ecstatic, fecund, alive as passionate love."[4]

Need something more technical and footnotey? (Like I should show my work, right?) Well, I've got one word for you: *perichoresis*. Think of it as a kind of battle cry for a new breed of theologians who are once again taking up the doctrine of the Trinity. Thinkers like Moltmann, LaCugna, and John Zizioulas (ziz-ee-ooh-las) are taking up influences from the East and bringing that groove home. Here's an ultrasimplified way of understanding their work: The West has focused too much on *person* and not enough on *relationship*. Worshipping the majestic "personhood" of God has yielded a modern God who is, in one way or another, an "absolute subject," a sort of great big one of us.

However, if we peer in upon the Godhead through the lens of the event of the cross, what we get is *perichoresis*, a living, active, circulating love that inheres between Father, Son, and Spirit. It's a love so mighty and active that, like a euphoric three-year-old spilling her apple juice, it overflows its rim, creates this world, and when things go horribly wrong, works *within history* to counter and overcome our rebellion. By leading with *perichoresis*, this self-circulating love, we ground ourselves in Trinitarian history: the suffering love of the event of the cross in which the Father is present and the Spirit is moving.

---

3. Jürgen Moltmann, *The Trinity and the Kingdom* (San Francisco: Harper & Row, 1981), 240.
4. Catherine LaCugna, *God for Us: The Trinity and the Christian Life* (San Francisco: Harper & Row, 1991), 1.

And one more thing. What this does for our understanding of *faith* may blow your little mind. Faith is not assent to and agreement with an absolute subject. Faith is not simply about morality, about trying to be good. Faith is not about our "experience" of the sacred (whatever that means). If this *perichoresis* stuff is real, faith is a living, moving, relationship that we are *taken into*. Moltmann is channeling this thought when he speaks of knowledge of the Trinity as "doxological," or to put it in a really simple way, "worship based."[5] Have you ever been a temporary atheist? And you stumbled into a church one day, and while the sermon might not have been that great, when you listened to the pipe organ and prayed the prayers and received the Eucharist, you sort of actually *believed*. You, my friend, have encountered this doxological awareness of divine relationship. It's a relationship that comes and gets you. Like a ride to the airport from your friend, the Spirit will be there around eleven o'clock to pick you up. The burden to believe is lifted. It's not about us and our ability or inability to believe. It's a matter of trusting that this event of the cross, in which the suffering love of the Father is present, emanates a living relationship that is coming to get you—and not just you, but all of creation. (Just try that with an apple. I dare you.)

And how convenient: this all points neatly ahead to our conclusion.

Conclusion: Implications of an Unfinished Event

Let's quit the Church of the Absolute Subject. Monotheism? Who needs it? The Absolute Subject presides over the Church of the Absolute, in which everything is based on fear. But the event of the cross is truly liberating. Here we have *permission* to *die*—to go down into the water and come back up to find that everything

---

5. Moltmann, *The Trinity and the Kingdom*, 152.

has been altered by the suffering love of God that radiates from the cross. Let's do it Trinity style. Let's get physical. Because history happens and matter matters. And this still-unfolding crucified presence of God in the world is a source of boundless, creative hope. Not escapism, but real, historical hope that even in the face of Empire, our dream of relationship is not a cruel joke.

And just as the perichoretic love of the Trinity spills over into the world, so also our hope spills over into this community. We become brothers and sisters, not through shared sublime experiences, not through trying to be better than each other, but through the blood of the cross. We are gathered, taken, folded into this relationship, each one of us: young and old, believers, half-believers and unbelievers, even those who have gone before us and are now more direct witnesses to God's pure love. We are one, in the blood of the Father's suffering love, the Son's trust in God's new way, and the Spirit that emanates from this event and whispers it in our ears and breathes it into our lungs.

May the triune God of grieving love, trusting obedience, and creative joy break us down, liberate us all, and bind us together as sisters and brothers. That we might receive the Word in all its freedom, disturbance, wildness, and beauty, and then proclaim this good news in ways that respect the freedom of the gospel and the integrity of the hearer.

3

De-Greekifying the Divine, or How to Quit *Thinking* about God

Dear Christians,
Please quit thinking about me.
Love,
God

Warning: In this chapter I will not be trying to prove that God exists. I'm just trying to tell you that something happened.

If I Only Had a Brain

Let's begin with *thinking*. What are you thinking about right now? Are you thinking about God? I mean, it couldn't hurt, right? After all, you are reading a book about theology.

Is God thinking about us? At the same time? Dude! Wouldn't that be weird? Does God have a brain—a really, really big brain? Like, if you collected up all the thoughts that humans are thinking right now, would that somehow equal some percentage, however minuscule, of what God is thinking?

To say that God "thinks" seems absurd. But why don't we find absurdity in *our* attempt to think about God? Can we really approach God with our brain? Oh, we're all guilty of it at times; those late-night, end-of-the-party, Chardonnay-inspired kitchen discussions about whether we can know if there is a God or not. As if we can think our way through it, as if our thoughts about God's existence somehow correspond to God's thoughts, as if our brains are the key to unlocking God's brain.

It is, as they say, the modern condition. Modernity has conditioned us to think about everything—to think too much.[6] And this whole modern condition has certainly influenced our approach to God. We've been trained to *think* about *God*. We end up trying to somehow connect with God through thinking: thinking big thoughts, big, enormous, complicated thoughts about morality, or transcendence, or why the ocean's near the shore.

Let's call this the "Greekification" of God, hearkening back to Plato and company, who divided the cosmos into substance, "stuff" (what's here), and "form" (the realm of the ideal). Plato was not wild and adventurous like the earlier so-called primitive philosophers. Plato was more nervous than that. And he dealt with his anxiety by *thinking*. Behind what we see, he reasoned, is some sort of order. "There's got to be some sort of universal mind behind all this mess," he reasoned, "creating order out of the chaos that we see." And like stink on a monkey, this dualistic way of thinking has henceforth tainted our Western understanding of God. Due to the heavy influence of the Neoplatonic thinkers who

---

6. Like I said in chapter 1, we've gotten pretty good at a certain kind of reason: instrumental reason. You know, the kind you use to make tools. We're pretty darn good at tool making. Maybe too good, right? Like, who knew our underarm deodorant in the convenient little spray can would deplete that layer of ozone that we sort of need? Here's hoping that us MacGyvers can all work together to find new tools to fix the damage from our tools.

first interpreted the faith, we've been led to believe that we ought to approach God with our brains instead of our bodies.

The Greekification of God yields the modern notion of *religion*. As if an isolated self can look within, discover the essence of *religion*, and then order his or her world according to it.

Rightfully so, this heady, brainy, and idea-based notion of religion has drawn much criticism. And God bless the pagans and neo-pagans for reminding us that we are not simply brains and ideas—that we are, after all, *bodies* in time and space who live in relationship with all other creatures and all of creation. Modernity bequeathed to us this dualistic bifurcation of world and God. And even when the atheists came along and banished God from the picture, the dualism still remained. The philosophers still relied on this idealism that held all things together, with humans at the center. In other words, even though atheists kicked God out of the system, they kept the system intact; they retained this confidence that the universe, science, language, and even the social world somehow correspond to the human mind.[7]

But what if the God of the Bible doesn't think at all? What if that has nothing to do with this God?

The God Who Happens

The God of the Hebrews, the God of the Jews, is very different from the Greekified God. This is not a God who exists in some other, transcendent realm. This is a God who comes here and *does*

---

7. A case in point is the Vienna Circle. These mathematicians in the 1920s seriously believed they had cracked the code, that they had forever solved the mystery of the universe by *proving* that our words correspond with objects in the world. Thus, reality could be really and truly known, through our language. Hence, language becomes scientific. Words and objects in the world correspond with each other, because of mathematics. What is, is all there is. And we can figure it all out. And then we die. (For a fascinating account of a philosopher who rejected mathematical certainty and became a critic of the arrogance and control of modernity, read the works of Ludwig Wittgenstein.)

things, a God who *happens*, a God who enters into our time and our history and leads us from here to there.

Moses, the first great leader of the Hebrews, was nothing like Plato. Moses did not become the leader of his people because of his exceptional IQ. He didn't think his way to the divine. According to the Hebrew Scriptures, this God simply showed up, in the form of (get this!) a burning bush. And this voice, purportedly the voice of the god Yahweh, pouring forth from the talking, emblazoned shrubbery, told Moses this: "I have observed the misery of my people . . . I have heard their cry. . . . I know their sufferings"[8]

This God could not be more different from the universal mind of Plato and the Neoplatonists. The Greekified God is about order, perfection, the transcendent—ideal forms of which our reality is but a shadow. But the Hebrew God, Yahweh, is messier. This God is reckless, passionate, empathic, and eminently relational. This God hears the cries of the people and decides to enter into the suffering, the ambiguity, and the painful pangs of historical liberation.

Now, as the story goes, this messy, empathic God appeared to Moses and chose him to be a leader, to tell the people that they would be set free from their misery. But then (according to my paraphrase of Exodus 3:7-15) Moses had the nerve to talk back to this God: "But suppose I go and talk to my people? Who should I say sent me?" In other words, "Who are you?" And God answered, "Tell them 'I am' has sent you." Or, better yet: "I am who I am." Or much more true to the Hebrew verb tense, "I will be that which I will be." Or to paraphrase even further: "If you want to know who I am, follow me and find out."

"Follow me. That's my name. Because things are going to happen."

The ancient Hebrews did not sit around and argue about whether or not God exists. They did not *think* their way to God.

---

8. Exodus 3:7, NRSV.

This God *happened* to them, appeared to them, made them sweet promises about their future—promises it took them centuries to understand.

They didn't think their way to this God; they waited for this God to reappear and lead them to the next place. And while they waited, they did something very important: they remembered what God had already done for them. They met together at feasts and festivals and prayed and worshipped and told their children what God had done for them. They remembered.

The Greeks—namely, Plato and the Neoplatonists—attempted to think their way to God. This implies that God can be known as an idea, removed from place and time and stuff, removed from the created world. But the God of the Hebrews is the odd God, the particular God, the historical God, the God who liberates, the God who delivers the people from slavery.

This God hears the cries of these tribal people, living as slaves under Pharaoh, and God delivers them, chooses them. And it does seem odd—to us and to them. To complicate things even further, it appears to have taken the Hebrew people a long, long time to figure out what it meant to be chosen by Yahweh.

In fact, it is not until centuries later, during the exile, that the prophets like Isaiah began to raise these bold questions: God chooses the Jews, but for what? Does God choose this people for war, for conquest, for domination? Were they supposed to conquer all their neighbors, defeat them in battle? Were they supposed to have a king like the other nations and an army like the other nations? Does being chosen mean that God will fight for them as they battle their enemies? Isaiah questions it all.

What if the people are *not* chosen to rule the world? What if the people are chosen to suffer, to cry "injustice," to be the reed that bends but does not break, to be the candle that flickers but will not go out? Yahweh, God, this odd God, points to *these* people, to these humiliated and powerless and broken and suffering ones and says:

Here is my servant, whom I uphold,
> my chosen, in whom my soul delights;
I have put my spirit upon him;
> he will bring forth justice to the nations.
He will not cry or lift up his voice,
> or make it heard in the street;
A bruised reed he will not break,
> and a dimly burning wick he will not quench;
> he will faithfully bring forth justice.
He will not grow faint or be crushed
> until he has established justice in the earth;
> and the coastlands wait for his teaching.
(Isaiah 42:1-4)

The covenant is *not* exclusively between the odd God and this particular people. They are to incarnate and enflesh and embody and then extend the covenant: "I have given *you* as a covenant to the people, a light to the nations" Yahweh says (Isaiah 42:6, NRSV). They are to *become* the covenant.

Is there a choosing, a particularity that is not exclusionary, violent, or oppressive? Is there a choosing that is radically destabilizing, expansive, creative, and gracious? That's the *radical particularity* Isaiah is pointing to. Through this one people, God chooses all the peoples. Israel is a gift to the world. Israel's chosenness is not for itself but for others.

The Greekification of Christendom

Now, through the magic of our imaginations, let's transport ourselves into the present. In our contemporary musings about "the existence of God," have we not, even us good Christians, almost completely Greekified God? Have we not turned God into a thought, an idea, a concept, a moral foundation?

The Bible does not profess a general notion of a general God. There is no such thing as God in general. Greekifying God yields various philosophical attempts at a general need for the existence of God as a foundation of some sort or other: God as first cause or God as the foundation of morality or God as the source of sublime religious feeling. But at its best, the Christian faith confesses a *crucified God*—God present and real in the event of the cross. This changes everything. It means that the deliverance and liberation of godforsaken humans lies in the figure of the godforsaken, crucified Christ.

There is a huge—a monumental—difference between thinking our way to God and confessing that God has done something. And whether you can believe it or not, let's at least be clear about what Christians confess. We confess that the Word became flesh and lived among us, that the glory of God is in these wounds, that God is here, in these nail-scarred hands of Jesus, that this light of suffering love shines in the darkness and the darkness will not overcome it. Christians confess that this same Jesus loved us, and taught us, and confronted us in our darkness and greed and self-obsession. God has chased all over creation and history to find us. And *hearing that word* is quite different from *thinking about the existence* of God.

It's time to de-Greekify the Christian God. We cannot think our way to this God. This God comes to us, just as God did to Moses and to Paul, and this God asks us to die that we might be born again. It is not simply the case that this God is irrational, or even a-rational. It's just that we cannot think our way to grace. Grace does not fit. Grace is the rupture, the incongruity, the surprise that we do not initiate, that is too good for us to ever think up. Grace is the homecoming we did not expect. Grace is the gift we find at our doorstep when we thought everyone forgot. Grace is the relationship that not only loves you now but also loved you into being and will love you beyond death.

An Antidote to Thinking about God: Paul's Hope for the Mending of Creation

Is there an alternative to thinking about God? Perhaps the best one is found in the biblical notion of *tikkun,* a Hebrew term that stands for, roughly, the mending of creation. Even in the midst of his persecution by the Roman Empire, the apostle Paul did not seek escape in another world. No, Paul boldly proclaimed his faith in God's *tikkun,* God's mending of creation. Paul didn't ask to be taken out of the world. Neither did he condemn this flesh. Rather, he yearned for the transformation, the redemption of the world, *this* world: "We know that the whole creation has been groaning in labor pains until now; and not only the creation, but we ourselves, who have the first fruits of the Spirit, groan inwardly while we wait for adoption, the redemption of our bodies" (Romans 8:22-23).

The spirit of the crucified Christ is here. Not up and out of this world, but here: giving birth, contracting, crowning, dilating, delivering God's gracious judgment. And the Spirit is working to transform the here-and-now world in which we live.

According to the apostle Paul in the brilliant and soaring eighth chapter of his Letter to the Romans, there's an important way for us to connect with this groaning of creation, this hope in the midst of hopelessness. It is not through thinking great thoughts. It's through prayer. Perhaps, just maybe, the proper alternative to thinking about God is prayer, prayer that is a sort of groaning and hoping with creation.

Prayer is so accessible. It is quite the opposite of thinking big transcendent thoughts that only a few—those who possess the secret knowledge or the biggest brains or the best education— can access. Paul could not go more out of his way to make prayer seem more accessible or available. We have simply to open our hands and receive.

The Spirit "helps us in our weakness," Paul writes, "for we do not know how to pray as we ought." But the Spirit "intercedes for us with sighs too deep for words" (Romans 8:26). In other words, prayer is quite the opposite of thinking sublime thoughts about God. Prayer is letting go of our differentiated, clutchy-and-grabby selves and receiving our identity as selves-in-relationship because of how radically God has come to us and to the world in the incarnation of Christ. Prayer is a response to something that happened, to what God has done, a response to the crucified and risen Christ, who calls us to die that we might be made alive. Prayer is a radical reorientation of those who have died with Christ. They have tasted death, they accept it, and yet they live again. They have renounced everything, yet they have taken it all back again, accepting the created world as a beautiful and holy gift.

According to Paul, "We do not know how to pray as we ought" (Romans 8:26, NRSV). This is the beginning of prayer, the door opening, the only way to start. Prayer is not about strength and power and self-assertion. It is about yielding, confessing, receiving, in the spirit of the tax collector who prays, "Lord, be merciful to me, a sinner" (Luke 18:13, NRSV) or the confession of a worried, pleading, parent in the Gospel of Mark: "Lord, I believe, help thou my unbelief" (Mark 9:24, KJV). For Paul, prayer begins and ends not with our ambition, but with God's grace alone.

This letting go of control, this admission that "we do not know how to pray as we ought" opens us to the upside-down, disturbing, broken, undone way of God: the way of the cross. In Jesus, the Christ, God has emptied Godself into creation, into our world. God is not removed from us; God is suffering with creation, groaning with creation, in labor with creation. God is on the bed in the birthing room. The spirit, the wind, the breath of God, is right there with us.

We are human—stubborn, arrogant, self-obsessed, self-negating, overly optimistic, overly pessimistic. But in the resurrection of the crucified Christ, something has happened. Our ineptitude cannot negate it. Our flawed attempts to think our way to God cannot negate it. Our embarrassing and even tragic mistakes cannot negate it. Something has happened, and now everything has changed. And instead of simply thinking, we can do so much more: we wait, we remember, we work, we love, we pray.

Like I said before, I am not trying to prove that God exists. I'm just trying to tell you that something happened.

4

Jesus Has a Question for You

WHO DO YOU SAY that I am?"[1] It's a question that Jesus of Nazareth put to his followers. And now it is a question that this writer will put to you: Who *is* Jesus?[2]

Most readers of this book will recognize that Jesus was a good guy, a *really* good guy. Whoever the historical Jesus was, there is ample evidence that his teachings and actions and parables were downright revolutionary. Jesus had a passion for turning the tables, for loving the unlovely, for touching the untouchables, and for teaching his followers to love and forgive even their worst enemies. And Jesus, while committed to peace, was not passive. He confronted the people in high places in the name of a nation oppressed by the terror and violence of the Roman Empire.

Who was Jesus? A good guy? A lunatic visionary who threw himself into the Roman machine? A zealot? Was he a divinely inspired prophet on the level of the Buddha or Muhammad?

---

1. Matthew 16:15, Mark 8:29, Luke 9:20, NRSV.
2. Please don't take this question in a shaming or manipulative way. I am all for honest, lively, and open discussion of the question. Some of my best friends are atheists.

41

The Gospel of John makes a rather extreme claim: that Jesus is, in fact, God with us, God incarnate, God made flesh:

> In the beginning was the Word, and the Word was with God, and the Word was God. He was in the beginning with God. All things came into being through him. . . . What has come into being in him was life, and the life was the light of all people. The light shines in the darkness, and the darkness will not overcome it (John 1:1-3a, 4-5, NRSV).

Was Jesus the incarnate presence of God, God with us, God made flesh? The big, bold claim of John the Evangelist is that God dove deeply into creation, into a world filled with violence and darkness, into sweat and sinew, into blood and bone.

Christology: The Question of *How*

How can this be? How can the man Jesus of Nazareth also be the Christ of God? A particular human being, in space and history and time, *and* God—in the same person? This has been one of the most divisive questions in human history, with answers that often provoked stern rebukes, banishment, and even bloodshed.

Today it seems absurd that humans would fight over such matters. We are grateful that in most parts of the world, a dissenting answer will no longer get us killed. But the purpose of this book compels me to burrow into this complex historical argument in the name of grace. What does this topic look like when viewed through the lens of relationship, namely, the Trinitarian self-giving love of Father, Son, and Holy Spirit?

For us to carry out this recovery mission, it will be helpful to review some of the issues that Christians struggled with in the first four centuries of Christian history. Lucky for you, I will help this ancient medicine go down by wrapping it in a spoonful of sugar—a tasty little discussion of my long-lost friends, the existentialists.

What Ever Happened to . . . the Existentialists?

They were our heroes, our revolutionaries, our knights in not-so-shining armor: the existentialists— Sartre, Camus, Marcel, Kierkegaard. They taught us not to try to get the right answers but rather to love the questions.

They shot great big holes through all the certainties, all the systems, all the empty platitudes of normalcy and success. Their "what's the point?" attitude actually kept us from wanting to start our careers. They inspired films that decades later expressed our post-college angst. Who can forget Ingmar Bergman directing Max von Sydow as the knight of faith playing chess with death, all in glorious, grainy, shadowy black and white? They inspired pretentious prog-rock bands to write songs about death. Nowadays, if you obsess about death, you have to be all smart and smarmy and ironic about it.

The existentialists had a saying: "Existence precedes essence." Damn straight it does. That means you begin with you and with your real life and your very real death. There is no pre-existing "essence" that your life must conform to. There is no system, no prescribed pattern. The raw immediate fact of you, your existence, precedes any kind of conceptually ascertained, preexisting essence.

In other words, you don't construct a system with your brain and then move inside and live in it. Our striving for order, for a system, is as comic as it is tragic. While our brain is out constructing these perfectly decorated mansions of sublime thought, our bodies are living in the doghouse in the backyard.[3] Existence is not orderly. We have to face our freedom, our finitude, our brokenness, our death. What does it all mean?

---

3. Søren Kierkegaard, *The Sickness unto Death* (Princeton, NJ: Princeton University Press, 1983), 13.

Whatever happened to the existentialists? These days, everything is, you know, "po-mo"—postmodern. Oh, I do grant the basic and obvious postmodern objection to the existentialists: they didn't go far enough; they forgot about the self. They questioned everything, except for the *self* that asks the questions. They left the self, the individual, the existential hero, in control. They didn't see that the self itself was part of the system, part of modernity's grid of control, conformity, calculation.

But it was the existentialists who blazed the trail. Have some respect for your elders! There would be no Jacques Derrida without Jean-Paul Sartre; there would be no Amy Winehouse without Aretha Franklin; there would be no Napoleon Dynamite without Screech.

What ever happened to the existentialists? I heard Martin Heidegger is appearing at Mystic Lake Casino. Kierkegaard is doing cruise ships. Gabriel Marcel is working children's birthday parties and bar mitzvahs. And Albert Camus has recently been featured on VH1's *Behind the Music:* "Scarred from a heroin-related bus accident that took the life of his publicist while they were on tour in Europe, but not content to live in the past, Camus has recently been in the studio again. And he swears his new material is going to be, and I quote, 'the best work I've ever done.'"

I want to bring the existentialists back. Not for a nostalgia reunion special that will air as a public-television fund-raiser. No, I seriously believe they can help us with this matter of Christology, of how we are to understand Jesus of Nazareth as both human and divine.

But first of all, the backstory.

Dead-Ending Our Way to Orthodoxy: A Brief History of the Chutes and Ladders of Christology

Christians confess that the historical figure Jesus of Nazareth is somehow "the Christ," "the Savior," "the Messiah"—that by uniting humanity with the divine, Christ changes what it is to be human. For the first couple of centuries, during the honeymoon period, Christians seemed more or less content to let the mystery be. *Somehow* Jesus was God in the flesh, God with us and for us. They didn't get too bent out of shape trying to explain just how this could be.

But pretty soon, the dirty dishes and laundry piled up, they had some trouble with the in-laws, and they began to argue over just how Jesus could be both human and divine. What they learned, through a series of dead ends, was what they did *not* want to confess. Here are a couple of things they did not want to say:

- They did not want to say that Christ had a human body with a divine mind or soul. They rejected this notion that the divinity part did not touch the human body parts. This maintained the crucial understanding that the Jesus of the Gospels got tired and thirsty, was afraid, was tempted, didn't always know exactly what he as going to do in advance (depending on which Gospel you're talking about), and as a baby, kept his parents awake at night and repeatedly soiled the divine swaddling cloths.
- They did not want to say that Jesus had a divine nature and a human nature that were somehow separated. Thus, they had to demonstrate good boundaries by disagreeing with Theodore of Mopsuestia, who claimed that the divine nature didn't taste the trial of death on the cross but, like teenagers at the mall with no money to spend, only hung around nearby. Theodore called each of the natures "he," which made it sound as if he was really talking about two persons. Contra the Gospels, in which we never sense that Jesus is some sort of two-member committee. From this dead end, we learned that the unity of the human and the divine in Christ had to be strong enough that Christ was one agent.

Now fast-forward to the Council of Chalcedon (451). When the leaders of the church (at least the ones who got invited) gathered there, they affirmed:

> We all with one voice confess our Lord Jesus Christ one and the same Son, the same perfect in Godhead, the same perfect in manhood, truly God and truly man, the same consisting of a reaonsable soul and a body, of one substance with the Father as touching the Godhead, the same of one substance with us as touching the manhood . . . to be acknowledged in two natures, without confusion, without change, without division, without separation.[4]

See how this contrasts with the views rejected:

- Against Alexandrian extremes: Christ was not a divine soul or mind plunked down inside of a human body.
- Against Theodore and those of his ilk: Christ's two natures were joined "without division [or] separation."

Please note two important instincts that the Council of Chalcedon followed:

1. They stated what the church ought to affirm, but they didn't offer a lot of explanantions about *how* that could be the case. Here, they took a stroll down negative lane: the two natures are "*without* confusion, *without* change, *without* division, and *without* separation." These negatives drew the line against potential errors, but they did not claim to penetrate the mystery far enough to understand just how it all worked.

2. The basic argument is that in Christ there were two *whats* and one *who*. If we ask who Jesus Christ was, there are two answers: he was God, and he was a human being. But if we

---

4. Council of Chalcedon, "The Definition of Faith of the Council of Chalcedon," in *Creeds, Councils, and Controversies*, 3rd ed., trans. C.A. Heutley (Grand Rapids: Baker Acedemic, 2012), 405f.

ask who did these things, there is just one answer: Jesus
Christ did them.

Existentialist Nostalgia Reunion Tour, Featuring Cruise Director Douglas John Hall[5]

It's kind of exasperating, right? Trying to wrap your head around
this Christology stuff? That's why I'm calling in the existentialists. Let's put them to work. It'll make them happy. And it might
just help us figure out this Christology stuff.

I called up a theologian friend of mine from Canada, Douglas
John Hall, and we went to pick them all up in his minivan. And
under the direction of Captain Hall, I asked them to teach me
about Christology. Here's what they told me.

First things first, they said. Jesus as both human and divine
is not some arcane belief that is imposed upon the Bible by the
subsequent tradition. The big question of Jesus' identity is right
there, as perhaps *the* fundamental question. The characters who
pop in on Matthew, Mark, Luke, and John are forever asking,
"And who *is* this?"[6]

The most extreme expression of the question comes near the
end of the story, as Jesus makes his so-called triumphal entry
into Jerusalem. According to Matthew, "the whole city was in
turmoil"; the *whole city* was asking the question "Who is this?"
(Matthew 21:10, NRSV). But here's the kicker: it is also the question that is put by Jesus himself: "Who do *you* say that I am?"[7]

There are little glimpses of an answer all along the way. But
the impression that the Gospels give is that the question is more
prominent than any of the answers. To the tradition of orthodoxy,

---

5. This chapter was inspired by Douglas John Hall's "Christology: The Identity of Jesus," which makes up section 28 of his *Professing the Faith: Christian Theology in a North American Context* (Minneapolis: Fortress Press, 1993), 370–94.
6. Ibid., 370.
7. Matthew 16:15, Mark 8:29, Luke 9:20, NRSV (italics added).

the tradition that tried to nail down this relationship between divinity and humanity, the answers have seemed so important. No doubt, the answers in the story are important. Especially the answer of Peter that follows the "Who do you say that I am?" of Jesus. Peter answers, "You are the Christ, the son of the living God" (Matthew 16:16, NRSV).[8]

But even this confession by Peter does not put an end to the question. That answer is immediately forgotten and contradicted by the disciples. Peter himself betrays Jesus in a painfully conscious sequence. And at the end of the story there is still an overwhelming sense of interrogation, both in the minds of the disciples and in the expressions of the communities that authored these books. *Who is this?*[9]

But we don't like being interrogated. We are not comfortable with not knowing the answers. So we try to lock it up and put it in a formula. The history of Christology is a history of answers to the Christological question. But the biblical answer is to *accentuate the question.* Ortho - doxy, "proper belief," tries to answer the question. But the Bible turns it up, amplifies it, throws it in our face. The relentless questioning of the Bible suggests that to answer this question is the beginning of a process of reductionism that the Bible itself somehow warns against and that Jesus himself somehow feared.[10]

The question of who Jesus is just might be the center of the New Testament record. Can the question of Jesus' identity even be answered? Must not Jesus remain, in some basic way, the unknown one, the stranger, the outsider, the one whose story remains unfinished? What if this was a very conscious move? What if the first disciples and their communities were sophisticated enough to know that as soon as we think we know Jesus, we have begun to dispense with him?[11]

---

8. Hall, *Professing the Faith*, p. 370f.
9. Ibid., 371.
10. Ibid.
11. Ibid.

I mean, really, if Jesus walked up to you and asked, "Who do you say that I am?" what would you say? I, for one, would not rattle off those words from the Chalcedonian council: "You are two *oosias* (persons) in one hypostatic union, without confusion, without change, without division, without separation."

There is a deep and wide tradition of divine encounter in the Bible, especially in the Hebrew theology of naming, of the name. The God Yahweh, who becomes present to the people, will not allow God's self to be named, even though the humans always demand to know God's name.[12] The name God reserves for those who come closest to God is a name that reveals and conceals at the same time: "I am who I am," or more acurately, "I will be that which I will be," or better still, "If you want to know who I am, follow me and find out." This God is a verb; this God is in motion.[13]

Do you like it when people define you? What if they tried to describe your nature? If I meet you and get to know you, I hopefully will treat you with understanding and respect and have the modesty and honesty to recognize that you are the other and must remain an other. If I define you, I objectify you—I treat you as an object, an "it." Our relationship is then finished. The center of the mystery of you has become an extension of my own mind and will; the "thou" has become an "it," a graven image of my own making, no longer free, no longer capable of calling me into question, no longer capable of loving me. Likewise, if our Christology does not point us back to relationship, it becomes an idol.[14]

Jesus is at the center of our faith not because he gives us answers, but because he turns up the questions, the big questions, the ultimate questions. What would this Christ be to us if he simply gave us the answers? And what happens to this Christ when

---

12. Ibid.
13. Ibid., 372.
14. Ibid.

we reduce our living faith to a string of theological beliefs that must be defended?[15]

Are there really any good answers for our deepest questions? The testimony of the Bible is not a list of answers. The Bible is more a witness to the presence of an answerer, an answerer who often appears as a questioner.[16]

This is mystery, but not a raw and empty mystery. This is the mystery of God's reckless love, the mystery that causes us to wonder, "And who am I?" If Jesus is a question, a questioner, it is also true that he reveals things to us: our rivalry, our denial of death, our self-aggrandizement, our self-deception, our arrogance, our sin. But also our capacity for loving relationship.

Conclusion: In Praise of an Orthodoxy That Self-Destructs

The question of Jesus' identity should not come from a theoretical problem: how can a historical person be said to combine the essences of humanity and divinity? It must come from an actual encounter. If the Christology we set out on paper crucifies this living encounter, wouldn't it be better to toss it all in the flames?

And so when we approach this gift and task of theology, the trick is this: How do we think critically about our faith, about the church's prophetic presence in our world, and at the same time, make our theology self-dissolving? How do we make it all melt away by pointing us to the living God, the divine encounter, the voice that says, "If you want to know who I am, follow me and find out"?

It begins, as it always does, with remembering—remembering the one who interrupts our betrayal with the "given for you" of his body and the new covenant of forgiveness in his blood.

---

15. Ibid.
16. Ibid.

5

(Jesus Bonus Chapter)

Dear God: Why Couldn't Jesus Have Been a Girl?

So I sent this e-mail. To God. I know that sounds really corny and cliché, but I really did it, just for the heck of it. I sent it to god@gmail.com. I also tried god@canada.com (because I have a hunch that God might be Canadian). Here's what I wrote:

Dear God:

Why couldn't Jesus have been a girl? Quite frankly, it would have solved a lot of problems.

See, God, I'll tell you how it is around here. Women are leaving the church. Good women. Smart women. Strong women. And we don't know what to do about it.

We've got these really smart and critical-thinking women who are raising this very serious and important question: Can a male savior save women? Some have decided that Christianity is inherently and hopelessly patriarchal. One of their slogans is "When God is male, the male is God." Even the ones who've stayed behind seem to be suffering from at least a mild case of pagan envy.

Oh, they're absolutely right to deconstruct the history of patriarchy. The great theologians of the church, like Aquinas and Augustine, argued that only the male of the human species represents the fullness of human potential. They really and truly *believed* that nonsense. And it got ingrained into some of the ways we run the church. And that's totally not fair!

Of course, this is *not* what Jesus taught. But he was, you know, a *man*. And it seems like so many misunderstandings could have been avoided had Jesus only been born a girl.

How hard would it have been to make Jesus a girl? Why didn't you do that? I mean, it would have made an even better story. The "incarnation," as they call it, is a magnificent story: you, God, turned all the tables by showing up as a helpless, vulnerable baby, born not in a palace, but in a stable, born to peasants who were not the power-people, but the people on the outside. Think of how much *more* revolutionary it would have been had the baby Jesus been a girl!

I'll be waiting for your answer. I, for one, have not given up on this whole Jesus story. Not yet. But I'd like a little help here. If you can't make Jesus a girl, at least help me out with a good and convincing answer to this question.
Sincerely,

Rev. Mark Stenberg
Mercy Seat Lutheran Church
Minneapolis, Minnesota

ıııııııııııı

I didn't know whether or not to send it. But I figured I might as well be honest. This really is a question I have, and I'd like an answer. So I e-mailed God about it.

Should I have done that? That's the problem with e-mail. Once you hit Send, there's no going back. How will God take it? Will it hurt God's feelings? Will it make God feel bad? What if God has no answer? What if no one responds?

I'm sorry to drag you into this little dispute. But I'm really struggling with this question. In working through this topic of the incarnation, I've run into a lot of these objections. In fact, one of my very favorite feminist theologians has written that Christology "has been the doctrine of the Christian tradition that has been most frequently used against women."[1]

Also, some portions of the Gospels, these stories of Jesus, can be centered on what the men do. Take the story of Jesus' birth. Sure, Luke inserts the gorgeous song of Mary (the Magnificat) into his story. But in Matthew, the story of Jesus' birth is quite androcentric; it is told pretty much entirely from the male perspective. The story is all about Joseph. He is the hero in the story because he decides *not* to have Mary put to death when he discovers she's pregnant. Joseph is held up as the virtuous one, the one who obeys. We get next to nothing about poor young Mary, who did all the work.

So. Back to the e-mail. I did get a reply. Do you want to see it? It's kind of crude. I don't really know if I should put it in print. And no, it was not God who answered it.

It turns out that, much as the post office, when it receives letters to Santa Claus, refers them to various charitable organizations, many Internet service providers transfer e-mails addressed to "God" to volunteer religious and mental-health organizations. My e-mail was answered by someone at the "Institute for Free and Un-coerced Faith," or I-FUF. I know nothing of this person, except for his nickname, "Lewis" (at least, I assume that's a nickname).

---

1. Rosemary Radford Ruether, *To Change the World: Christology and Cultural Criticism* (New York: Crossroad, 1982), 45.

From the tone of the e-mail, I can't help but try to imagine who Lewis is. I'm guessing he's got a good handle on theology but is lacking in certain social graces that are necessary for face-to-face interactions. Frankly, he seems kind of grouchy.[2] Well, perhaps if I show it to you, you can judge for yourself.

⁣⁣⁣⁣⁣⁣⁣⁣⁣⁣⁣⁣⁣⁣

Dear Reverend Stenberg:

Your e-mail of 12/14/14, addressed to god@gmail .com, has been forwarded to us. Please understand that, here at the Institute for Free and Un-coerced Faith, (1) we assume no legal liability for our response; and (2) we do *not* speak for God. These conditions being understood, please allow me to respond to your query.

1. Mark, I think you have some serious issues. I mean, who died and left you king of defending the faith? Look at you, trying to "defend God." La-di-da. Do you think God needs you to light his cee-gar? Trying to defend God, to "clarify God's position," has been a very dangerous impulse. It assumes that *you* know best. And then you're only one step away from locking everything all up in your own little private enclave of proper belief, in which you alone have passed the test.

This God is alive. Moving. Stripping us of these idols we keep trying to build, some of them in God's name. Of course, patriarchy is a serious problem, one that's still with us. But don't let your battle with your enemies remove yourself from the whole big thing—the great big love that sweeps away *all* of our idols. It's alive. Don't try to kill it.

2. So you've noticed that Jesus is a male. Good for you. But have you ever noticed that he's also *Jewish?* You've

---

2. You might find it helpful to read his answer in the voice of stand-up comedian Lewis Black. That's who I had in mind when I invented this chapter.

never noticed this whole particularity thing before? And how offensive people find it? How could God choose the Jews? Doesn't that seem unfair to everyone else? Unmodern? Unenlightened? Exclusivist?

But presenting the question that way is backward. It tries to stuff the history of *this* God's dealing with *this* people into some ethereally constructed Platonic box, built on the scrap heap of our speculative questions.

Jews *and* Christians claim that this is something that *happened:* that God, Yahweh, heard the cries of the slaves in Egypt and delivered them. This God saved them, liberated them, chose them. But, this God of particularity chose them for a purpose, for a reason. They were chosen to be a nation of priests to the other nations. They were chosen to serve, to liberate, to spread the love. Get it? Through their particularity, all particularity is to be affirmed and blessed. This is the God of creativity, not conformity.

Quit trying to *think* your way to something that *happened*. What are you doing, writing a term paper? The Bible tells us that this liberation is happening. It's not so big on speculating about why it happened in this way.

If you get to know the guts of the Hebrew Bible, it claims two things about this particular, choosing God: (1) this God is mystery; and (2) this God is reckless love. Of course, thinking critically about your faith is important. Faith seeks understanding. But don't let your speculation snuff out the mystery, through which this reckless love of God must take apart our idols, for the sake of something better.

You might wish that Jesus had been born a girl. OK, I could go one better and wish that Jesus had been born a dyslexic Lithuanian diabetic. With asthma. Or an effin' dolphin for that matter, so that his perspective could include a nonhuman critique. Or even better than that, on behalf of the poor and oppressed inanimate objects everywhere, I could wish that Jesus had been incarnated as the Formica tabletop at booth number two at Chang O'Hara's bar. But the point is that God is *with us*. The point is to see this particularity not as a curse but as a blessing.

3. Regarding the book of Matthew: Do us all a favor and use your imagination once in a while. Read between the lines. Learn to spot the code language.

A quick example: The wise men brought the baby Jesus *myrrh*—a death spice, used for burial. In the entire history of baby showers, has anyone ever shown up with a more inappropriate gift? "Uh, here, Mary and Joseph, we brought you some embalming fluid, just in case." What could be more inappropriate? Or more obvious to Matthew and this community of believers, who see things way beyond and outside of the text? It tips you off that these were dangerous people who lived in a dangerous time. They didn't have the luxury of asking sophomoric speculative questions about God. They were on the fly, on the run. Running for their lives from King Herod.

And regarding the Gospel of Matthew, I will grant that it's a tough one for us to hear. It's the most particular, the most Jewish, of the gospels. But if you learn to crack the code a little bit, it's also the most fun.

And for that matter, go back and really look at Jesus in all the Gospels. They are stories of *conflict*, stories of an upside-down kingdom in which the religious leaders are hypocrites who have it all wrong, and the outcasts of society— prostitutes, tax collectors, and Samaritans—are able to hear the message of the prophet. And this reversal of order is not simply a turning upside down of the present hierarchy. It aims at a new order in which hierarchy itself will be overcome.

In the Gospels, Jesus ministers especially to outcast women, not because he somehow wants to embrace "the feminine." He does so because they are at the bottom of the network of oppression. And Jesus the liberator will continue to embrace the underside, to serve and empower all those oppressed by racism, sexism, classism, homophobia, and whatever other oppressive social structures we humans might invent.

4. Jesus was a particular human being. But was he really a "male"? Not in the sense of these gendered roles that we create. Yes, men and women are created differently, particularly. Jesus was male in this way; we must not emasculate him. But *gender*, this social role that we play, this code that we think is written in stone, is a social construction.

Pardon my rant. But this gender role thing is getting worse all the time! Have you been to your local big-box discount store and walked through the toy section lately? Santa brings boys loud and violent toys, while girls get sweet, sexy princess toys. We've taken God's good diversity and made it something that divides and separates. But gender—our cultural webs that define our roles as women and men—*that* is a cultural construction that ought to be challenged. And Jesus *did* challenge it. Look it up.

5. Pastor Mark, have you ever heard of the "offense of the gospel"? I thought so. But you gotta watch out. There's a bad way to understand it and a good way.

"The offense of the gospel," bad way: There are limits to reason. Reason only takes you so far. At that point, you need to take a leap of faith. You even have to accept things that are an offense to reason.

"The offense of the gospel," good way: The word of God burns. The mystery, the reckless love—it's not something we can conjure up from within. And when it comes, it leaves a mark. It stings and burns. But this offense is radically "for us," as the theologians say. The offense takes all our carefully constructed idols, the images of God which are often merely projections of us, and topples them, for your sake. And for the sake of *us*—you and me and our relationship with each other.

6. Your position, Pastor Mark, is dangerously close to fundamentalism. Do you know what a fundamentalist is? A fundamentalist is someone who is critical without being self-critical. And just because you're a bleeding-heart pinko lefty doesn't mean you can't be a fundamentalist, too. We get e-mails all the time from fundamentalists of the left.

So if you agree that you can't be critical without being self-critical, you have a question to answer. What *is* your source of self-critique? Can anyone, anywhere ever kick your skinny white ass? Shake you up? Tell you that you just might be deluded, misinformed, misguided, or in any teeny tiny way *wrong?*

That's the beauty of Christian ethics. (Not that anyone notices anymore.) This Christian ethic, properly understood, is a *grace* that *judges* us. We have this uncanny source of self-critique. There is a *no* to our ways of destruction and dis-relationship that is only spoken for the sake of the *yes* of restoring us to God's relationship of perfect love.

7. The story is not finished. It's alive. And what you do is a part of it, even now, after two thousand years.

I expect a deep subversion of all our notions of gender, of what is male and what is female, and a judgment upon all the ways we dehumanize each other through our classified social roles.

What's more, I expect a blessing of our particularity, our diversity, and a mending and a fulfillment of the creativity that God showed in starting up the whole thing.

Respectfully yours,

Lewis

‖‖‖‖‖‖‖‖

I didn't know what to make of it. It kind of made me mad at first. And I still wish that Jesus had been born a girl.

But it also made me happy. Like it's not my job to defend God. Like I can trust the Spirit to open things up in ways that I could never have imagined.

There is a place to give it our best shot—to give our most intelligent, engaging, and creative response to our faith in God's mercy, love, and justice grounded in grace. But there is also a time and place to simply let go and receive. To eat and drink this liberation that God has begun.

6

Why Your Theory of the Atonement Sucks

How DOES IT ALL work? In chapter 4, we looked at the person of Christ and tried to make some sense out of the question "Who is Jesus?" As a counterpart to this question, we now examine what Jesus *does*. Jesus saves, but how? What does it mean that two thousand years ago, this homeless Palestinian Jew was put to death in a very public show of torture by the Roman Empire? How does that event reconcile us—make us one—with God?

"Atonement" is actually a sixteenth-century English word that was put together from the words *at, one,* and *ment*. At-one-ment. Atonement. Because some way, somehow, Christians believe that the cross of Christ makes us "at one" with God. But what does the cross really mean? How does it work?

A Warning: Our Constantinian Infection

Before we approach this subject, we need to cleanse our palate, to start over, to wipe the slate clean. There's an obstacle that obscures the deep meaning of the story of the cross. Whether we like it or not, we Americans are used to being the imperial power. We are used to seeing a cross on top of the highest building in town. The cross is not an embarrassing part of the story for us. In a way, it represents our triumph, the triumph of a cultural Christendom that has far too often trafficked in materialism, wealth, money, and power.

But for many of the first Christians, the cross was an embarrassment. At the center of the story was failure—in fact, not just failure, but a grisly, horrifying murder, which today no parent in their right mind would allow a child to watch. Jesus was lynched by a mob.

Some of the early Jesus followers were embarrassed by this story. It made them look like total failures. How could that crucifixion even be in the story? It made absolutely no sense to their wealthy and successful Greek and Roman neighbors. It was a failure story, and they were first-class fools for believing it.

Here's just how embarrassing the cross was. There arose a strain of Gnosticism that denied that the Christ, the Messiah, ever had a human body. His body, they claimed, was just an empty shell. The real Jesus left his body before he was ever crucified, because that sort of failure cannot happen to the Christ, the Savior. But as the story began to sink in, brilliant followers of Jesus, like the apostle Paul and the writer of the Letter to the Colossians began to absolutely insist on the incarnate, flesh-and-blood facticity of the death of Jesus, which they viewed as the center of the story. But before we get to that, we've got a pesky problem to deal with—namely, the history of various *theories* of the atonement.

Theories of Atonement

As moderns, we have this fascination with theory. We love our theories: chaos theory, decision theory, phlogiston theory, elimination theory, quark, ring, and set theory. We have theories about everything. We have theories about theories. That's because we're really quite good with our brains and our information, and we have utmost confidence in the knowability and fixability of all things.

In all sorts of various and diverse disciplines, theories work. Sort of. They are a form of shorthand. One of my mentors defines a theory as "a string long enough to tie up all the facts."[1] But the danger with inviting our theories to church is that they threaten to take over, to become a substitute for the real thing—the actual story that the church tries to hear and tell and enflesh in the world, the story of this event that actually happened. Again, we've gotten a bit lost in the realm of idea, concept, and theory. We are too much in our brains and not enough in our bodies—too much in the realm of ideas instead of in this flesh, this matter, this time, these events, this story that happened two millennia ago.

Why should we bother knowing about these theories of the atonement at all? Wouldn't we be better off without them? I mean, who cares?

That attitude would be fine, except that the church has already been contaminated. In our context, there has been one theory of the atonement that has become all too pervasive, to the point at which, for many Christians, it has become the only way to talk about the cross.

The (I Can't Get No) Satisfaction Theory

The "satisfaction theory" of the atonement, otherwise known as "substitution" or the "penal substitution theory" (shout it out loud, I dare you), has been woven right into the fabric of the contemporary Evangelical Christian culture. Some of us grew up

---

1. James William McClendon Jr., *Systematic Theology: Doctrine* (Nashville: Abingdon, 1994), 213.

with this theory, and we know it quite well. To state it in a rather crass and ungenerous way, the theory goes something like this: We humans have been bad—very, very naughty. We have sinned against a righteous and holy God. God's reputation has thus been besmirched, and God's righteous wrath has been set in motion. Where does this divine wrath end up? It would all be directed at us—full-force judgment—except that, wonder of wonders, Jesus, our older brother, steps in. He takes the beating, the punishment, the righteous wrath, so that we can get off the hook with our angry father.[2]

The great benefit of this theory is that it's easy to tell. It's a convenient shorthand account of God and Jesus and us. We can turn it into a tract and make it an evangelism tool. In fact, to date, over sixteen million "four spiritual laws" tracts have been printed in one form or another.

However we might try to soft-sell it, at the center of this theory stands the *wrath* of God—a God who turns against his son, Jesus, and thus severs (at least temporarily) the relationship of Father, Son, and Spirit. But according to the story, these Gospels of Matthew, Mark, Luke, and John, is that really what happened?

Liberal Media Bias

The liberals, bless their little hearts, have recognized the wrath-of-God stuff in this theory, and in a classic case of penal-theory envy have presented—or rather revived—a different ancient theory, one that we can trace back to the great scholastic, Peter Abelard (1079–1142). In the "moral-influence theory" of the

---

2. If you want a richer and more generous take on this theory, go back to Anselm (1033–1109) and read his *Cur Deus Homo* (Why did God become man?). A true saint and the archbishop of Canterbury, Anselm was one of the highest-ranking church officials to formally denounce the Crusades.

atonement, Jesus is more than simply a substitute, a stand-in who shoulders the blame. No. The whole point of the cross is to bring an "inkindling of charity," a demonstration of love to human beings who have lost their way.

Here Jesus is the example of full personhood. He is self-actualized, whole, perfectly integrated. Jesus was no hypocrite. He took his cause to the limit, to martyrdom. He is the "vicarious sacrifice" who draws us into his love so that we might have the strength to love others.

According to the moral-influence theory, God is like a perfect, loving parent. Jesus, God with us, is our moral exemplar, our teacher, our rabbi. The human problematic is not that we are mired in sin. Our problem is that we are ignorant of real love, enslaved to lies and deceptions. But we are capable of reform, given the right nurture and training and education—*lots* of education. Liberals love that.

My one beef with this theory is its overly optimistic reading of the human condition. It's too straight-line, too once-born, too let's-climb-up-this-ladder-to-God, too confident in our reformability. With this theory, it's balloon Sunday every Sunday. Relax. Have a cookie. Things aren't *that* bad.

But what if we are a lot more lost and broken than that? What if what we need is not reform, but rather revolution? To go all biblical on the bit, doesn't this theory seriously deny the core message of Jesus, that in order to be born again, we first of all have to die? Doesn't it do an end run around the basic biblical message about the human proclivity toward idolatry—our penchant for creating God in our own image, for making God into a great big one of us?

As a counter to the satisfaction theory with the wrath of God at its center, the moral-influence theory is understandable. But it really doesn't work as a substitute for the real story. Again, it's theory and not story. It's in our brains; it's not something that happened.

Meanwhile, over in Lund . . .

In an odd case of academic discovery, there was a mild-mannered Swede named Gustaf Aulén, who happened upon and recovered one more ancient theory of the atonement, the Christus Victor theory. According to this theory, evil exists, in ways we don't even know. Were it not for the cross of Christ, which has set in motion the victory of good over evil, we would all be swallowed alive by Satan. The cross represents God's victorious triumph over the forces of sin, death, and the devil. In the cross, something really happened. The cosmos has been restored and rescued, and the Holy Spirit is working in us to overcome the dark powers of the world.

According to this theory, God is the triumphant warrior who must defeat evil. Human beings are oppressed, not just born into original sin, but oppressed by the dark forces. We cannot simply *enlighten ourselves* out of the darkness. Sin is a supra-personal force that has a composite, concrete existence.

How can these liberal do-gooders be so arrogant and smug in the face of evil? Evil exists, in ways we don't even recognize. We are oppressed by the powers and principalities.

Even though this theory can sound sort of primitive and dark, you have to admit that it does, at least, move us into the realm of promise and future. Also, for my money, one of the most blessed lines in the creed has always been, when speaking of Jesus, "He descended into hell."

It seems the most useful of the three theories, provided that (1) we never turn this into an us-against-them or insiders-against-the-outsiders narrative; (2) we resist the dualism it can foster—like there's this secret world behind our world, and that's the only one that really matters; (3) in the light of the ever-decentering cross, we resist the triumphalism that places the church over against the world; and (4) the violence in the language of the cross is understood, as it often is in Paul, metaphorically.

And speaking of metaphor, it's time for an English lesson.

Before There Were Theories, There Were Metaphors

The Bible doesn't give us *theories* of the atonement. The Bible speaks about the meaning of the cross by means of metaphors—scads of metaphors, all kinds of metaphors.[3]

If a theory is "a string long enough to tie up all the facts," a metaphor is something like a contextual device for speaking the truth in plain language. A metaphor draws upon two (or more) sets of associations and usually refers to a model or models. Metaphor is intentionally mixed-up speech.[4]

In Shakespeare's play *As You Like It*, the Duke is trying to comfort his band of exiles, banished to the Forest of Arden. He praises the forest for its

> books in the running brooks,
> Sermons in stones, and good in everything.[5]

Proper speech would place the stones in the brook, and the sermons in books. But the Bard mixes it up with metaphor.

"This chalupa is heaven."

Get it? I threw together two dissociated things and made them both refer to the model of tasting something that gives me pleasure.

"My tricked out Ford Escort is a beast!"

"Mercy Seat Lutheran Church is the bomb!"

"Your soul is a golden butterfly gliding on a unicorn, riding across a ribbon of rainbow."

---

3. The author is indebted to the work of James William McClendon, especially the work he has done regarding the preference for metaphor over theory in our understanding of the atonement. See McClendon's *Systematic Theology: Doctrine*, 216–26 for a much more thorough analysis.
4. McClendon, *Systematic Theology*, 216.
5. Ibid.

A wise old mentor once taught me that in the Bible there are hundreds of metaphors for the atonement and that they can be organized into four classes, or clusters:

1. There are metaphors of law, regarding justice and judgment, punishment and substitution, which the Evangelicals draw upon for their favorite theory. If we remember that the early church was *against the law* in many parts of Rome, it's no wonder that the writers played with legal metaphors. But note that these metaphors can be read in a rather subversive way: According to Galatians 4, Christ was born "under the law" and "endured the law's full weight." And that's not just religious law. It's political. This guy was *lynched*—a victim of capital punishment, condemned in a hasty and unfair trial. The gospels are *against the law*, against the violence of Rome's law of might makes right. The cross exposes the corruption of the empire.[6]

2. There are metaphors of military victory, as the Christus Victor theory emphasizes. The cross of Jesus represents a triumph over opposing forces. He is victorious over the enemy. The earliest Christian confession is simply "Jesus is Lord." *Jesus* is Lord, not Caesar. These metaphors are capable of being downright subversive. They appeal to an upside-down power, a blessedness of the powerless, and the cross as God's subversion of empire power.[7]

3. There are metaphors of kinship and redemption. In our context, this cluster has really not been developed into its own theory, because it is so foreign to us. But the gist of this class of metaphors has to do with the fact that the Hebrews lived in a kinship network in which relatives could stand in for family members who were in trouble.[8]

---

6. Ibid., 217f.
7. Ibid., 219f.
8. Ibid., 220–22.

4. There are metaphors of sacrifice, upon which theories of Christ's sacrificial, inspiring love are based. The Hebrews took up the kind of ritual sacrifice that was common in many cultures. But they radically altered and twisted it. And their concept of sacrifice was dripping with meaning from the Passover, which commemorates the liberation of these slaves from their oppressors. The apostle Paul uses all kinds of sacrifice metaphors to describe the cross of Christ and, in fact, mixes them all together, so they evoke Passover, the Exodus, the Last Supper, all brought together so as to illumine the death of Jesus.[9]

So we've got all these metaphors. We can group them into four clusters: law, military victory, kinship, and sacrifice. And we can see how the various theories of atonement can appeal to these metaphorical strands. But were these clusters of metaphors ever meant to spawn their very own respective theories? Maybe this says more about us and our modern obsession with theory, with trying to make "a string long enough to tie up all the facts."

Metaphor Storm: Colossians 2:14-15

What makes me even more suspicious of these theories is that in addition to these four classes of metaphors (law, military victory, kinship, and sacrifice), there are also *mixed* metaphors. They get mixed together, wildly. This is particularly evident in Colossians 2:14-15.

What we have in this Colossians passage is not a theory of the atonement but rather metaphors that attempt to tell the story in a contextual way. In this little letter to the Colossians, when Paul (or whoever wrote the book) talks about the cross, there are little outbreaks of metaphors—crazy, mixed-up metaphors—for talking about the cross.[10]

---

9. Ibid., 222f.
10. Ibid., 226.

Let's break down the metaphors captured in just these two verses from the letter:

> When you were dead in trespasses [in sin] . . . God made you alive together with Christ, when he forgave you all your sins:
>
> (1) erasing the handwritten record that stood against you,
> (2) setting it aside,
> (3) nailing it to the cross,
> (4) stripping the rulers and authorities,
> (5) putting the rulers and authorities on public display, and
> (6) gaining a victory over those rulers and authorities in the cross.

I want us to look at three of these little metaphors in the cluster: stripping the leaders, the handwritten record, and the public display, or parade, of the defeated.

Stripped

One of the wilder metaphors is that term "stripped," often translated "disarmed." (The cross strips or disarms the rulers and authorities.) Many historians think that when Jesus was crucified, his clothes were taken from him. The shame of public nudity was a deliberate part of the humiliation of a Roman crucifixion. This makes the metaphor "stripped" even wilder: the rulers and authorities thought they were stripping and exposing Jesus, but in reality, they were the ones stripped and exposed as the enemies of God's peace, who are being defeated by God's forgiveness, the peace of the cross.

The Handwritten Record That Stood against Us

A second wild metaphor snack tells us this: at the crucifixion of Christ, God took our "record of sin" and "nailed it to the cross." The term for "record" here might have meant signatures collected by loan sharks, a politically incriminating document in one's own handwriting, a handwritten certificate of debt (an IOU of some kind) or a cosigning for which the signee is held responsible. Well, according to this wild letter in the Bible, this very record of our sin has not only been taken away, it has actually been nailed to the cross by God.

And the readers of the letter recall the sign that Pilate put on the cross: "This is Jesus of Nazareth, King of the Jews." The Romans meant it as a cruel joke, because the Jews were so despised. But the secret meaning of the act was that, unwittingly, Pilate himself was making this confession.

Jesus is the King of the Jews, the Messiah of God's people, and this is how the King of the Jews is getting across his message of suffering love and forgiveness and resistance to the empire's violence. In that moment when Pilate's officer nailed this declaration of Jesus' guilt to the cross, God nailed to the cross this "record of our sins"—the record that is true because it contains our sins, but is no longer valid because, in the cross, God forgives our sins.

The Mercy Parade

But the best, wildest metaphor here has to do with a parade, a procession. When the Roman emperor would conquer a new city or territory, defeating its army, the emperor would set up a victory parade. It was utterly twisted and cruel. He would gather all the defeated and conquered soldiers, civilians, women, and children, line them up in a parade, and drag them down Main Street to show off the victims of his imperial might. So cruel. Sociologists have labeled this a "status degradation parade." We can hardly imagine a more atrocious display of the "might makes right" of the empire: ritualized humiliation in which the defeated were mocked and ridiculed and laughed at by the imperial rulers.[11]

---

11. For a richer and even more vivid interpretation of this text see René Girard, *I See Satan Fall Like Lightning* (Maryknoll, NY: Orbis, 2001), 137–53.

Jesus of Nazareth was in one of these parades. Pilate condemned him, and the soldiers forced him to carry his own cross through the streets. And that parade is the reference for this wildest of metaphors: "At the cross God disarmed the rulers and authorities and made a public example of them, triumphing over them" (Colossians 2:15, NRSV).

God made a public spectacle of them, leading them as captives in his triumphal procession. How's that for a really twisted metaphor? The "conqueror" leads his "captives" in a "triumphal procession." This beaten, homeless Palestinian Jew, who has been abandoned by all his followers, drags his cross through the town square while everyone laughs at him because he's such a failure and because God has, apparently, *abandoned* him.

That is the triumphal procession to the cross. Through this— human shame, embarrassment, failure—Jesus enfleshes God's love. It is the great subversion of love over against violence. The divine peacemaking of the cross involves not only the violence committed against Jesus in his death but also the gracious overthrow by God of these powers, these "rulers and authorities." The rulers and authorities seemed to win the battle against God and Christ on Golgotha, but in fact, they were the ones who were defeated.

⸻

So back to our big question about the cross: What does it mean? It means too much—so much that can't be captured in a theory. Better than any of our theories of the atonement are these wild metaphors that can't be systematized. And better still than these metaphors themselves is their ability to drive us back to the story, the story the church attempts to proclaim in the preacher's halting, piecemeal words every week. The story that is enfleshed, taken into our bodies, in this great feast of the Eucharist, the great thanksgiving for God's radical peace, forgiveness, and justice grounded in love.

In the end, the atonement is nothing but the good news of relationship. Though the violence parade seems in full gear, it has already been overcome, undone, broken, by the cross of Christ. It has been stripped of any lasting power. Our sins have all been nailed to the cross, and we can all get in line, behind Jesus, in this parade in which we are taken captive and shown off as the ones who are defeated and conquered by God's love. Welcome to the peace parade, a joyful procession that pronounces the defeat of the violence of the empire.

7

Holy Spirit Revival, Featuring Live Snake Handling

Look, let's be honest. We've done an appalling job teaching about the Holy Spirit in the contemporary church. The doctrine of the Holy Spirit is all fuzzy and spooky and ghosty. Or it is simply ignored. Or it is used as a question of doctrine, as a tool for attacking our opponents, rather than a living word that can reveal the self-giving nature of God.

I'll admit I'm no expert here. In fact, I'm convinced that there are people who know a lot more about the Holy Spirit than I do.[1]

---

1. I truly do believe that there are people who know a lot more about the direct experience of the Holy Spirit than I do. We call them Charismatic or Pentecostal Christians. And while there is a great diversity among them and it's rude to make generalizations, they do share a belief in a more direct and visceral presence of the Holy Spirit that manifests in such gifts as speaking in tongues and prophecy and healing. And no, I cannot simply write them off as crazy, because they have had a profound effect on so many for whom the Word had become stone. I very much consider them my brothers and sisters in Christ. It's just that these experiences are so foreign to me that I'm afraid I'm going to refrain from further discussion because I simply can't give them the insider description they deserve.

So please temper what I say with your own experience. But I'm also convinced that I have something important (dare I say prophetic?) to tell you about our understanding of the Holy Spirit and the current state of spirituality in general.

In this chapter I will begin by laying out the seriously gnostic condition in which we find ourselves using a couple of very personal examples. *Gnostic?* Please relax. I'll walk you through this very carefully. Next, I will attempt to recover a Trinitarian understanding of the Holy Spirit by linking the Spirit more directly to Jesus, the Christ. The chapter will end with a meditation on the Apostle Paul and his breath-taking vision of *tikkun*, the *mending of creation*, as found in the eighth chapter of his Epistle to the Romans.

The State of the Holy Spirit Union: Fuzziness, Confusion, and a Whole Lot of Gnosticism

In our time and place, one of the most serious distortions of the faith is our gnosticsm. Gnosticism is a broad and general word for those strains of thoughts and beliefs that in one way or another devalue the meaning of the physical world in the name of some sort of *spiritual* otherworldly realm. A very important strain of early gnosticism actually denied that God created our world. This strain of gnosticism would regard the created world we live in as a sort of mistake, a failed attempt—created not by almighty God but by a demiurge, a sort of junior god, a god-in-training. Thus, they would recommend that the solution, the fix, is to transcend this world through various practices that more directly connect human souls with the realm of pure spirit that transcends the created world of matter and biology and flesh and blood.

The church has never been completely free of this gnostic temptation. Somehow, we've gotten the idea that "spirit" takes us out of the world, that spirit is opposed to matter, to stuff. We cling to this notion that our spirit is like Casper the Friendly

Ghost inhabiting our body—that we somehow have a tainted, corrupted body that is nothing more than a vessel for the pure, clean, happy good spirit that lives inside each one of us.

That's the problem I have with *spirituality*. On both the right and the left, there are current notions of spirituality that completely take us out of the world of flesh, of creation, of history, of matter, of time. The goal of these pop spiritualities is to transcend, to escape, to take us away, and to ascend. However, if there is one thing I want to do here, it's to move spirituality into the realm of flesh and bone.

An Excursus Regarding Two Items I Received in the Mail While I Was Grieving

With your permission, I'd like to take a rather abrupt turn. Think of this as a curious little excursus on what happens when a bookish, nerdy, academic, decidedly anti-gnostic Christian theologian tries to make sense of his grief. Oh, and it does have very much to do with the Holy Spirit. I promise.

On March 19, 2007, my dear spouse, Natalie Retamoza, the love of my life, to whom I was married for sixteen years, died of colon cancer. Within a month of her death, I received two anonymously sent items in the mail, both in plain manila envelopes with no return addresses, both lovingly intended to provide comfort in the midst of my grief.

The first anonymously sent item was a poem, ordered and sent from a website called Heaven's Roll Call. The poem is entitled "Tears." The theme of "Tears" is that Natalie is up in heaven, waiting for me. The poem explains that the tears I cry are memories, sent to remind me of my love for Natalie:

> Do not stop the tears you cry
> For they're sent from God above.
> They're not a sign of weakness
> But a representation of your love.

The poem then assures me that each single tear I cry corresponds perfectly to one memory that Natalie and I had together. It also assures me that we will meet again. And it all ends with the triumphant theme that death is simply the "graduation of life on Earth":

> Death is a graduation of life on Earth
> And the memories are the tears.
> Each tear represents a moment in time
> That will last throughout the years.
>
> Now close your eyes and be at peace
> And know you'll meet again.
> God loves you so. He won't let go
> And His grace will never end.

Now, please understand. I am so very grateful for the intention behind the gift. It was an honest attempt to provide comfort. And there is a kind of sweetness to the poem that makes me not want to disparage it and go all highbrow on it and critique it for crowding in these clumsy five-syllable words like "representation" when it's obvious that "symbol" or "likeness" would have done just fine, thank you very much.

But regarding the gift and the task of theology, of taking a step back and figuring out how to best proclaim the good news of the gospel of Jesus Christ, my real problem with the poem is that it is so up and out of this world. In this poem, spirituality is pretty much about transcending this world, this dreary life on earth, from which we will soon graduate. Spirit bounces off the crust of the earth, ricochets off our soil, and hovers over us without diving in. The Holy Spirit doesn't reach into us—into our skin and flesh and marrow, into our lungs, livers, hearts, and guts. Life here on earth becomes empty, a stage, a play from which we will graduate when we die and go up and out of our flesh, up and out of our bodies, to be with Jesus in heaven. This turns the Holy Spirit into a cloudy, misty, vaporous, friendly ghost of Jesus, who hangs around here, in Jesus' absence, but is here only to escort our souls up to the pearly gates of heaven when we die.

The second anonymously sent item I received was a book, James Van Praagh's *Healing Grief: Reclaiming Life After Any Loss*.[2] (I have a feeling that these two items were *not* sent by the same person.)

Van Praagh has sold millions of books. Oprah and her legions are all over this stuff. However, in spite of its popularity, the book is really not that bad. In fact, it has probably helped a lot of people through the grieving process by encouraging the bereaved to own their "negative emotions" and "not deny and repress them altogether."[3] Van Praagh offers some very practical wisdom regarding the grieving process. In the midst of a culture heavily steeped in the denial of death, he offers real insight regarding the variety and the volatility of grief.

It is not my goal to condemn this book. Rather, my point is this: I received these two well-intended items in the mail, both sent anonymously, as ways of offering comfort in the midst of grief. But they both missed the mark because, to some extent, they both attempt to provide comfort by taking us *out* of this messy world, by transcending what is here—matter, history, time, flesh, relationships—in the name of an *out* and *up* and *above it all* spirituality.

The "Tears" poem does this in a more obvious way by subjecting everything in the flesh to second-tier status and making spiritual reunion in heaven the goal. But Van Praagh's *Healing Grief* also does this. It turns history into an illusion. It recommends a transcendence that is up and out of this world.

When the body is shed and we cross over to the spirit world, we open the door to eternal life. It is there that we discover

---

2. James Van Praagh, *Healing Grief: Reclaiming Life After Any Loss* (New York: New American Library, 2001).
3. Ibid., 4.

that we are spiritual beings having human experiences. You will find through the stories presented in this book that we are on this earth to evolve and develop spiritually. In order to do so, we make choices before incarnating into our physical bodies to place ourselves in various situations in order to grow.[4]

According to Van Praagh, in the process of grieving, "you are playing your part to evolve to the next phase of your spiritual development."[5] This world of flesh and blood and skin and bone and plants and animals and matter is regarded as merely a stepping stone to our soul's evolving spiritual journey—a higher consciousness that connects to a realm of pure spirit that is detached from the present earthly reality.

These are both heartfelt, earnest attempts to provide comfort, to deal with our losses. But, speaking both as a grieving widower and as a theologian of the church, I find that both of them miss the mark because they are too transcendent, too esoteric, too up and out of this world.

Is There a Distinctively Christian Spirituality?

You don't have to believe a word of it (sometimes I don't), but let's at least be clear about what it is that Christians confess about the Holy Spirit, and how this is the basis for *Christian* spirituality. Christians confess something very simple: that the Word became flesh and lived among us, that the glory of God is present in the wounds of the crucified and risen Christ. Christians confess that Jesus of Nazareth lived right here with us; he loved us, taught us, and confronted us in our darkness and greed and self-obsession. He told us that we have to die, to let go of our self, so that we might be born again as selves-in-relationship. He took all of our

---

4. Ibid., 7f.
5. Ibid., 8.

violence and hatred and became a victim, on our behalf. And God raised him from the dead in order to confront our violence and show us a new way to live.

There were humans, women and men, who saw all of this happen (we call them the "apostolic witness"), and they began to tell others about it, and they really did, for a brief period in time, turn the world upside down. And they have passed this message down to us. In word (speaking) and in sacrament (action), this long line of witnesses has, in spite of ego and drama and violence, kept this memory alive and handed it down to us.

The Holy Spirit is simply the Spirit of Christ in the world—here, in this flesh, with us. The Holy Spirit is not a cloud or a ghost. The Holy Spirit is the Spirit of the grief of the Father and the love of the Son that is here with us as redemptive, sacrificial, suffering love. Fleshy and earthy and bloody and messy, the Spirit is working "in, with, and under" creation to lure us toward redemption—here in our skin and bone, in our time, in our history.[6] And one more thing: regarding the fact that we are mortal, that you and I are going to die, the Holy Spirit is not a friendly ghost of Jesus, who snatches our souls and escorts them up to heaven when we die. No! The Holy Spirit is the Spirit of Jesus Christ who raises the dead. And that is a very different thing.

The Official Teachy Part about the Holy Spirit

There are plenty of sensible things to say about the Holy Spirit—sensible, orthodox Christian views that are helpful, grounding, and anti-gnostic. Take, for example the following "three aspects of the Holy Spirit," gleaned from some old lecture notes I found.[7]

---

6. Martin Luther, *Luther's Works: Word and Sacrament III*, vol. 37, ed. J. J. Pelikan, H. C. Oswald, and H. T. Lehmann (Philadelphia: Fortress Press, 1999), 306.

7. Looking at the Bible and the tradition, we can also make the following helpful (but sort of boringly orthodox) comments about the Holy Spirit. (1) The Holy Spirit is the spirit of the wounded and risen Christ. (2) The Holy Spirit is wind that blows Gods' grace to us. (3) The Holy Spirit is breath, the breath

1. The Holy Spirit Is the Spirit of Jesus Christ

At the end of the Gospel of John (20:22), Jesus breathes on the disciples and says, "Receive the Holy Spirit"! The Holy Spirit is the power of God that makes Jesus Christ real to us. It doesn't happen in a vacuum. It doesn't happen just for the sake of God the Father and God the Son. The Holy Spirit connects the Word (the message of God's love) to us. Humans get their share of forgiveness, reconciliation, resurrection of the dead, and eternal life through the Holy Spirit.

2. The Holy Spirit Is the Wind, the Breath, of Life

The Holy Spirit is the wind that blows from here to there. The Spirit is the breath of our mouth that goes from one person to another. God the Holy Spirit breathes into us in order to make us open and free and capable to receive the Word, as in creation, as in when Jesus breathed on the disciples. Humans need to be made ready for this. They are not ready for it already. They are not open to this naturally. They don't want to receive this. They openly or secretly trust in their ability to maintain order, to be in control.

The miracle of faith, of accepting mercy, is that we let ourselves be told that we not only commit sin but are sinners. This is something we cannot believe on our own. This is something that can only come from God. But it never comes apart from the word of God's love. That sinners can accept and believe is as big a

---

of God that fills our lungs. (4) The Holy Spirit makes possible the miracle of faith, of accepting mercy, of letting ourselves hear the ugly truth about us, but also the truth that God is with us and for us in ways too deep to understand. (5) The Holy Spirit is relationship—the overflowing love of the perfect relationship between Father and Son, who love in perfect freedom, expecting nothing in return but receiving everything back again. (6) The Holy Spirit is our comforter—this wounded, broken spirit of suffering love, who meets us in our darkest moments, who is present to us even when we can't feel it, who is most present in our weakness.

miracle as the resurrection. And it can only happen through this breath of God.

3. The Holy Spirit Is God

At the heart of the Triune God is relationship. The Father loves the Son and has from eternity. The Son loves the Father and has from eternity. Together, they love in perfect freedom, expecting nothing in return and receiving everything. Together, in this perfect relationship, is where the Holy Spirit lives. The Holy Spirit is the power that flows from this relationship: the spirit of adoption, the spirit of revelation, the spirit of witness, the spirit that makes us open to the Word of God.

꘏꘏꘏꘏꘏꘏꘏꘏꘏꘏꘏

Those points are all well and good and safe—and sort of boringly orthodox. But for my money, what we really need to counter this contemporary pop gnostic spirituality is a good ol' dose of crazy apostle Paul.

Let the Wild Rumpus Begin: The Holy Spirit and the Mending of Creation

And then there's Paul. Dear, crazy, subversive Uncle Paul. I know you've heard some bad things about him. But trust me, if you met him, you'd soon discover that he is about nothing but grace.

Paul's letter to the Romans is a wild thing. But whereas some theologians treat Romans as a treatise on justification by faith or a pastoral letter dealing with specific problems in the church, I see it as something much bigger, bolder, and more subversive. To me, the great theme of Romans is found in Paul's notion of *tikkun*, the mending of creation.Even more remarkable is the fact that Paul asserts these claims right in the teeth of the Roman Empire.

How could he possibly be so boldly optimistic about this foolish cross of Christ? It is truly staggering.

In the eighth chapter of Romans, Paul writes about the Holy Spirit, or to be exact, the human awareness of the Holy Spirit. In verses 18-27, Paul claims there are three things that assure us of the presence of the Holy Spirit, three things that are signs of life lived in the presence of the Spirit. These are not exactly proofs or arguments. They are testimonies, markers, signs along the way. Paul is not arguing. He is exhorting, comforting, and spreading hope like a virus.

1. The Spirit Is Present in the Groaning of Creation

It's easy to take Paul's language about "creation being under a curse" as a sort of crude and primitive mythology. But I think there's something more going on here. Creation is broken, bent, in need of mending. But maybe that's not through some arbitrary curse, some magic spell that inhabits our flesh like a virus. Maybe creation is cursed by human arrogance—by violent, self-obsessed, shortsighted human beings who think they are the center of all things. Creation cries out; it groans for deliverance. This groaning is the presence of the Holy Spirit, because the Holy Spirit is in the process of giving birth.

Paul relies heavily on this birth metaphor. The pain is real. You can't deny it. You can't drown it out. You can't escape to some other world. The contractions increase in intensity and in length. You breathe. You groan. You work the Lamaze—long breaths, short breaths, change the pattern. That's Paul's metaphor: "We know that the whole creation has been groaning in labor pains until now: and not only the creation, but we ourselves . . . groan inwardly while we wait for adoption, the redemption of our bodies" (Romans 8:22-23).

Note that the Holy Spirit is *here*. We don't leave home. Home is transformed. Spirituality is not a secret passageway up to another world. The Spirit is working to transform the here-and-now world in which we live. Yes, it's painful. But it's going somewhere. History means something. Matter matters. You don't pretend that suffering doesn't exist. You try to change it.

Is the created world a miscarriage? A sort of mistake created by a demiurge, a sort of junior god? That's what the gnostics were teaching in Paul's day. That was their answer to the pain and the violence they knew so well. But Paul could not be more opposed to them. For Paul, the Spirit is here, giving birth. The pain of miscarriage has to be one of the grimmest and most hopeless kinds of pain there is, utterly senseless pain that goes nowhere, that ends in nothing. But birthing pain is different. Yes, it hurts, but something is happening. Paul claims that this world is not a miscarriage. That the whole created world is in labor pains. That creation groans with eager longing. That it is moving toward *redemption* through God's liberating love.

And—again—it takes place *here*. The Spirit is *here*. We don't ascend to it. *It* comes to us. The Holy Spirit is not about our powers of spirituality. It's about God's grace. It's about this Spirit of God that is in labor pains, birthing something new, restoring creation to its glory.

2. The Spirit Is the Source of a New, Eschatological Force in the World: Hope

What makes Paul so confident? How can he believe this stuff about the mending of creation? Doesn't he see the Roman Empire? Doesn't he know the threat he lives under? The violence, the greed, the power of Rome? Paul wrote this letter to the believers in Rome, as a sort of letter of introduction. He had never been there. What he didn't know was that within five years, he would get to visit Rome. He would be taken there as a prisoner and executed. How could he possibly believe in this universal mending of creation?

Well, Paul had something that sustains and nourishes and empowers him. Paul has hope. He writes these quirky little lines:

> For in hope we were saved.
> Now hope that is seen is not hope.
> For who hopes for what is seen?
> But if we hope for what we do not see, we wait for it with patience.
> Romans 8:24-25a

Please, don't try to get all logical with that. Don't try to figure it out; it'll drive you crazy, maybe because here Paul's words point so completely beyond themselves. They point to the cross. Paul's impossible hope lies in the crucified one, in the impossible possibility of the cross.

For Paul, hope is not merely optimism. Popular culture seems to be driven by grand swings of optimism and pessimism. We get waves of optimism—over the stock market, technology, patriotism. "Play your cards right, and you can retire at forty and buy a yacht and cruise around the world." This optimism is followed by waves of pessimism over our violence and greed and destruction. "Sell all your stock now, build an underground bunker, and stock it with guns and single-malt scotch and dehydrated fruit."

But beyond optimism and pessimism is hope. Those who have died with Christ, those who have been baptized into Christ's death, have a different point of view. They have tasted death, and they accept it, yet they live again. They have renounced everything, yet they have taken it all back again, accepting the created world as a beautiful and holy gift. To die with Christ is to taste the curse, the death wish, the ugly truth about ourselves and each other, struggling for dominance. Yet, with Christ, we have been made alive again. We wake up and begin to approach each other and all creatures, not as objects to be consumed, but as beautiful, one-of-a-kind gifts.

Hope is not an anesthetic. It doesn't take us out of the world. We still suffer pain and loss. But this is the suffering of intimacy, of being connected and attached—to life and to each other, connected to a world full of violence, sickness, accidents, cancer, and death. It comes from being radically *attached* to this messy, fleshy, terribly beautiful world that God created and gave to us. And, of course, we still grieve. But as Paul says, we grieve, but we do not grieve "as others do who have no hope" (1 Thessalonians 4:13). Dying with Christ, we put the resurrection in God's hands. We wait for what is not seen. We hope.

3. The Holy Spirit Intercedes on Our Behalf

According to Paul, the Holy Spirit "helps us in our weakness; for we do not know how to pray as we ought, but the spirit intercedes for us with sighs too deep for words" (Romans 8:26). We don't know how to pray as we ought. For Paul, that is the beginning and the end of prayer. We begin and end with God's grace.

We are human. We are stubborn, weak, arrogant—overly optimistic, overly pessimistic. But the Holy Spirit intercedes for us, stands in the gaps for us, takes our side. The Spirit intercedes for us with sighs too deep for words.

Maybe in the end, our misunderstanding of spirituality is a misunderstanding of God. We don't get to God by transcending this world, because God is not a transcendent being. In Jesus, the Christ, God has emptied Godself into creation, into our world. God is not removed from us; God is suffering with creation, groaning with creation, in labor with creation.

Perhaps this intercession of the Holy Spirit works something like this. Out of the mutual love and trust between God and Jesus, the Holy Spirit flows, "spills out." Maybe this kind of intercessory prayer is the Spirit spilling out of this relationship and embracing our situation and returning again.

The intercession of the Holy Spirit? Think of your older brother who (occasionally) takes your side and protects you. Think of the arms of your mother, holding you when you've scraped your knee, or when you're sick, or when you burned your hands on the stove. Think John Coltrane at the end of the fourth movement of "A Love Supreme," his tenor sax groaning, wailing, praying, interceding on behalf of us and on behalf of our whole fallen world. It is crying/praying/interceding with sighs too deep for words. It is painful. It's a voice that has known suffering and loss. But it's also hopeful, fully convinced of the *redemption* of creation, of the resurrection of the dead, fully convinced that nothing can separate us from the love of God.

8

God and Creation: How I Got Over My Pantheist Envy

We now turn our attention to what theologians call "the doctrine of creation." You and I have somehow appeared on this planet, at this time, in this place. And though we can acknowledge that our Earth is only a tiny part of a vast cosmos, we cannot help but ask questions, the big questions, questions that shape our understanding of and our attitude toward our physical bodies and the body of the earth, questions about the world as we know it.

||||||||||||

Is the world beautiful? Or is the world tragic?

The beauty is all around. If and when you happen to notice, your senses are bathing you in beauty: the colors green and blue, the smell of lilacs outside your bedroom window, the taste of home grown basil in the red sauce you just made from scratch, the sound of a mother singing a lullaby to her child in the airport, the embrace of a good friend who you've not seen in years. You also have these tangible, personal gifts: this mind full of wonder and curiosity, this capacity for relationship—for giving and taking and forgiving, this ability to dream, to hope, to envision a better future—not just for you, but for *others*.

And yet you also know grief. There is violence in the world. Try as you might you cannot keep it at bay. You try to stay vigilant and responsible—to identify with the victims in your neighborhood, your nation, and your world. But sometimes it is just too much. And you also know loss. You've lost a friend, a parent, a child. You've been betrayed. You've been bullied. You've been drawn by your empathy into a situation that seems beyond hope.

Beauty on the one hand, grief on the other. For the faithful, for the half-faithful, even for those who have moved beyond, the mystery provokes primal questions about God and God's relationship to the world:

Is there a God? And if so how are "God" and "world" related? Is God above the world? Outside of the world? Is God watching over the world, from a distance? Is God "in" the world? Is there a "God" at all, in the classical sense, or is there only the world, aka the cosmos?

Be it known that the author does not endorse printed page resolutions for such matters. These—the most intimate and ultimate questions—cannot be solved in thought. There is no equation. The margins cannot be justified. To provide a simplistic answer would do an injustice to both the beautiful and the tragic. The resolution—if there is one—is bound to time, to future, to history. Only time will tell.

Nevertheless, in the name of theology, that task of stepping back and offering up a transient and temporary response for a church called to speak a word of grace, this chapter will unfold in three parts. In parts one and two I will examine, and ultimately reject, two of the classic, historical, inherited, models for understanding the relationship between God and the world. In part three I will speak of a third option as a way forward.

Model 1: God over and above the World

According to the first model, God stands over and above the world, up and outside of the world. This God is the supreme being who rules over the world. This God is transcendent, unchangeable, independent, invulnerable. The strangest thing of all is this: as familiar as this model might sound to those who grew up with this image of God, this is not really the God of the Bible. The source for this model of God is Greek philosophy. During the adolescence of Christendom, when Christian theologians were trying to figure out what it all meant, the biblical notion of God was kidnapped and hijacked and taken for ransom by Greek philosophy in the tradition of Plato. God was Greekified, defined in categories of philosophical absolutes. The transcendent aspects of the biblical God were enlarged and extended. God became eternal in the sense of utterly non-temporal (outside of time). God became necessary in the sense of absolute non-contingency. God became self-sufficient in the sense of absolute independence. God became changeless in the sense of participating in absolutely no change. God became purely *spiritual* instead of in any way *material*. God became unaffected by and thus seemingly unrelated and even un-relatable to the world.

In our context, belief in this God sometimes manifests a hyper-Calvinist notion of "God's will," a sort of secret plan, known only to the mind of this God, a will that is unchangeable and inscrutable. We humans cannot fully know God's will, not for sure. So we live in fear of taking a wrong turn. According to this image of God, *God's will* makes all things happen—even bad things, even tragic things. In this model, the way to comfort someone who has suffered a tragic loss is by telling them that "it was God's will." You affirm that there *is* a God and that God is *in control*. But at what price? What kind of God is that?

What is the meaning of life, according to this model? To get spiritual! If you are not being spiritual, *right now*, then you should feel uncomfortable, estranged, slightly ashamed of yourself. Life in the world is to be transcended. Matter doesn't really matter. History doesn't really happen. The created world becomes more or less an elaborate stage on which to play out the winning or losing of your salvation.

Who is Jesus, according to this model? Jesus descends and then goes back up to the clouds in order to pull a few of us out before the whole thing goes up in flames.

Model 2: Pantheism—God in the World with Nothing Left Over

When you grow up with the over-and-above-the-world God and you begin to realize how oppressive it can feel, pantheism, in any one of its several forms, becomes downright liberating. Pantheism *is*. What is, is what is. And what's wrong with that? Pantheism puts God in the world, with nothing left over. God *is* the cosmos—nothing more and nothing less. And what's so wrong with that?

You find yourself embracing and even reveling in the pleasures of this world. Sight and sound, touch and taste, music, poetry, laughter, food: you are no longer ashamed of simply being alive. If *everything* is divine, there is suddenly a sense of intimacy—of immediate, bodily, sensory pleasure in the world as it is given. That nagging, constant, back-of-your-mind suspicion that you don't belong here? Suddenly, all of that is gone.

And so you return to some of those books you were supposed to read in college, and you discover this little gem, written by William Wordsworth:

> The world is too much with us; late and soon,
> Getting and spending, we lay waste our powers:
> Little we see in Nature that is ours;

We have given our hearts away, a sordid boon!
The Sea that bares her bosom to the moon;
The winds that will be howling at all hours,
And are up-gathered now like sleeping flowers;
For this, for everything, we are out of tune;
It moves us not. – Great God! I'd rather be
A Pagan suckled in a creed outworn;
So might I, standing on this pleasant lea,
Have glimpses that would make me less forlorn;
Have sight of Proteus rising from the sea;
Or hear old Triton blow his wreathed horn.[1]

The poem catches you off guard, in the best possible way. Here you had been living your life in such phony piety—and such shame—and you didn't even know it. Always trying to measure up to some ideal, some standard, some internal voice of authority. And just like that, you are liberated. It is *enough*—to notice, to breathe, to be.

Freed from this culture of shame and fear you now revel in your senses. I mean, really: isn't it all just so beautiful? And who even notices? There is so much beauty surrounding us. And we become so selfish and distracted. Remember that moment, that breath, that entire day, when you simply *noticed?* You were not trying to be good. You were not even thinking of yourself. That walk in the woods? That time it snowed all night and everything was cancelled and you just spent all day playing in the snow with your friends? That night you accidentally looked up and saw the *aurora borealis* and you forgot all about sleeping?

Isn't it enough that we simply notice? Isn't it enough to really *taste* your food? To inhale and to exhale? Isn't it enough to be present, in this moment, in this breath—awake, aware, and alive?

---

1. William Wordsworth, "Sonnet XXXIII: The World Is Too Much with Us" (1807), in *The Works of William Wordsworth* (Hertfordshire: Wordsworth Editions / Cumberland House, 1994), 259.

How many days must we spend walking around in an unconscious stupor, getting and spending and crossing off lists? Isn't it enough to simply worship the day? Is the world all there is? And shouldn't that be enough? Holiness is here, all around us. Isn't it enough that we simply notice? Isn't it enough to worship—to worship this creation?

The Interruption

Violence.

How do we account for the raw fact of violence? Not just mistakes, or defense mechanisms, or aggression in the name of the survival of the fittest. But what do we make of the complex systems of violence that cause us to throw our hands up in the air and simply toss out the labels—"racism, sexism, homophobia, and exploitation"? We might try to pass off some of these violent acts as anomalies, as the result of genes gone bad, as aberrations that we hope to evolve beyond. But so many of these acts of violence seem to be deeply rooted in systemic ideologies: Matthew Shepherd beaten and bruised and hanging on a fence in the middle of the night in Laramie, Wyoming; Dylan Roof walking into a Wednesday night prayer meeting in Charleston, South Carolina, and gunning down nine African Methodist Episcopal church-goers who were praying for the healing of the world; Islamic militants torturing a school bus full of Pakistani Schoolgirls?

This, exactly, is the tragic. And it interrupts our peaceful Pantheist retreat. What do we do with the raw, in-your-face, fact of violence? Not just an accidental mutation of genes but entire systems that would hate and exclude and crucify the other? Pantheism, though it cultivates this awareness and presence in the world, cannot account for unspeakable acts of violence. It hears not the cries of the victims of history.

The Third Option: God as Radical Relationality

But what if, opposed to both these two extremes, there could be a *tertium quid*, a third option? On the one hand, the Greekified, "God over above the world" results in a denial of life, the flesh, the creation. On the other hand, Pantheism, "God in the world with nothing left over," cannot account for violence, for the victims of history. Is there a third way? What if God is relationship? Relatedness? What if God is outside of but also in the world, "reconciling the world to [God]self," as it says in 2 Corinthians 5:19 (NRSV)?

We don't need the God of the absolutes: unchanging, outside of creation and time above it all. Absolutes—they can't measure or describe relationship, which is what the Trinity is all about. But here's a radically different way of understanding God. It's from an ancient hymn to Christ in Philippians 2:5-8:

> Let the same mind be in you that was in Christ Jesus,
>> who, though he was in the form of God,
>>> did not regard equality with God
>>> as something to be exploited,
>> but emptied himself,
>>> taking the form of a slave,
>>> being born in human likeness.
>> And being found in human form,
>>
>>> he humbled himself
>>> and became obedient to the point of death—
>>> even death on a cross.

What is this? Where did this come from? This is the God who enters our world, our very flesh. We were looking for a fill-in-the-blank answer, but suddenly an entire landscape opens up. This is the God who comes *here*. This is the God who dives into creation. This is the God who suffers. This is the God who knows the violence from the inside out. This is the God who takes the side of the victim, all the victims of history.

We don't really need a God who is above and beyond it all. We don't need the absolutes. They are an invention of the Greek mind. We need relationship. We need hope. We need love. We need a God to be able to do something about the mess, the violence, the victims of history.

But that's backward—as if we could *think* our way to God.

So let's start over. Instead of trying to think our way to God, let's try to hear *what happened*, according to the Hebrew and Christian scriptures. The Hebrew Bible is about liberation. These tribal people are slaves in Egypt. They cry out for deliverance, and this God, Yahweh, hears their cries and chooses them—not for conquest, but for service, to be a light to the nations. And, in the spirit of this ever-expanding liberation, we can easily make the claim that this light shines on *all* of creation—not just human suffering and injustice but the darkness that we name in all spaces and places of our exploitation and violence against the planet.

The Christian scriptures, which include the newer testament, make a similar but even more audacious claim. They assert that God teased out the darkest part of us, our most violent, lynchifying, rivalrous part, and put it all on stage, for all the world to see, in order to confront us with it and overcome it, in the resurrection, the peaceful un-lynching of Jesus, the innocent victim.

According to the biblical witness, God is not "over and above" the world. Neither is God emptied into the world, without remainder. Rather, God is in the world, working out a salvation that is within history, within time.

There are a number of ways of talking about this:

- Process theologians (Open Theologians in Evangelical speak) talk about God luring creation forward, taking all that happens—the good, the bad, and the mundane—and transforming it, luring it forward, toward God's loving and just end. God works through the persuasive power of love and not through the coercive power of violence.[2]

• Liberation theologians, especially in the third world, speak of a God who can't be understood except in the context of real, historical liberation.

• The new Trinitarians speak of a radically relational God. The Trinity, they assert, is neither a concept nor a theory. Rather, it is bound to the old, old story of the cross of Christ. Its leading affirmation is that God is there, in the event of the cross.

⁕⁕⁕⁕⁕⁕⁕⁕⁕⁕⁕

We do not know where this is going. But we know where we've been. The distant, over-and-above-us God is not only inconsistent with the picture of Jesus the Christ who emerges from the stories of Matthew, Mark, Luke, and John; it is also downright toxic on a personal, social, and ecological level. Pantheism can be praised as a blessed and beautiful attempt to restore the fallen value of the created world. But, in the end, pantheism cannot account for cruelty, evil, and suffering—the tragic violence in the world that takes the lives of millions of innocent victims. And so this offering, this simple, contextual, transient, but hopeful alternative: *God is not over and above the world. Neither is God emptied into the world, without remainder. Rather, God is in the world, working out a salvation that is within history, within time.*

Like I said before, I do not believe that such matters can be worked out in words on a page. These—the most intimate and ultimate questions—cannot be solved by thought. The resolution—if there is one—is bound to time, to future, to history. Only time will tell.

---

2. I'm grateful to Jacob Erickson for his input on this chapter. Jake sounds the alarm and yet manages to offer up beauty and hope at the same time. I can't wait to see what he does next.

9

How to Read the Bible Backward

CONFUSING AND DIFFICULT BIBLE the find you do? Backward it reading try.

That Bible? Those two testaments? They were not written from the beginning to the end. Imagine these two testaments as a twin pack of delicious Hostess Twinkies. Two cream-filled treats wrapped in sponge cake that can sometimes taste kind of stale. People, go for the frosty cream filling inside! It's OK! Suck the middle out of it first![1]

Let's *not* start at the very beginning. It's *not* a very good place to start. When you read, you begin with A-B-C. When you sing, you begin with do-re-mi. When you read the Bible, you begin with the mercy.

---

1. Again, we've Greekified the Bible, just as we've Greekified God. The Bible is not a collection of ideas or arguments. The Bible is a record of stuff that happened.

Part One: The Hebrew Bible

Let's get right to the point. The core, the center, ground zero, the cream filling of Twinkie number one, the Hebrew Bible, is *liberation*—the exodus from slavery in Egypt. A very important text, from Deuteronomy, says, "When your children ask you in time to come, 'What is the meaning of the decrees and the statutes and the ordinances that the LORD our God has commanded you?' then you shall say to your children, 'We were Pharaoh's slaves in Egypt, but the LORD brought us out of Egypt with a mighty hand'" (Deuteronomy 6:20-21, NRSV). It's the single most defining moment for the Hebrew people. It's the center of the Twinkie.

Up until this point, they really didn't know that much about this God. There were primitive stories of giants and floods and this mobile God who often bailed people out. There were promises, early covenants, and renewals of covenants. But what defines this strange, mobile God of these ancient tribes is that this God has a heart. This God has soul. This God hears their cries and delivers them. They were slaves, and Yahweh set them free. The center of the Twinkie: God's liberation—not based on anything the people do, but simply because that's who this God is and what this God does.

The trouble is, these people were apparently quite forgetful. Even with this anti-forgetfulness strategy built right in, the people forget in some pretty serious ways.

It's the prophets, at the end of the story, who most clearly and vividly and creatively tell the people all the things they forgot. The prophets tell them how they, the oppressed, turned into the oppressor. Meet the new boss, same as the old boss. The kings of Judah and Israel turn out to be just as good at empire as old Pharaoh in Egypt.

The prophet Jeremiah rants and raves at the kings of Israel and Judah. Once upon a time, says Jeremiah, Yahweh planted a vineyard. But instead of yielding the rich red wine of peace, justice, and mercy, the vineyard yielded the bitter grapes of violence, oppression, and bloodshed. All along the watchtower, the princes feast, while the people go hungry (Isaiah 5:1-4, NRSV).

The Technique

Now, here's how you read this stuff backward. You go to the end of the great big story, and you put on your prophet goggles, you lock your brain into Isaiah- or Jeremiah-vision mode, and you look back upon the kings, this nation, and their conquest of the land. And you suddenly realize what a volatile, complex, and downright *tense* work of literature we have here—a literary body that is rich in internal dialogue, drenched in counterpoint between the prevailing powers and the critics, who speak from the underside of history.

There are these muddled stories of a muddled conquest of the promised land, in which we're never quite certain what is really the will of God and what is the people manipulating it all according to their greed or insecurity or paranoia. And then there are the kings who take over. In the name of power, in the name of national security, the stories of the kings are filled with jabs and heckles and barbs and downright accusations—that the kings usurped the role of the priests in the temple, that the kings silenced the prophets.

At the end of the story, the prophets suggest that the people are not chosen for conquest—that they never were. Yes, the people were chosen, delivered, rescued from slavery. But it takes a long, long time for the people to understand just why they were chosen. In fact, if you believe the prophets, it takes loss, ruin, rejection, judgment, sacrifice, and suffering to understand what it means to be chosen.

And by reading even those most disturbing texts backward, you suddenly are opened to a wondrous new world of hidden, codified critique, right there these texts! Who needs a new

conspiracy theory when we've already got this really rich codified language in the Hebrew Bible that you get by reading it
backward, through the lens of the prophets?

We can go to the heart of the matter by looking at a very
important text about why there were even kings in the first place.
Before any of the kings of Israel and Judah, all the elders gather
together and come to Samuel, a wise old judge, and they tell him:
"You are old, and your sons do not follow in your ways; appoint
for us, then, a king to govern us, like other nations" (1 Samuel
8:5). And the LORD says to Samuel (with more than a hint of sarcasm), "Listen to the voice of the people . . . , for they have not
rejected you, but they have rejected me from being king over
them" (8:7). "Only, please," he adds, "try to warn them."

So Samuel tries to warn them: "These will be the ways of the
king who will reign over you: he will take your sons and appoint
them to his chariots and to be his horsemen, and to run before his
chariots. . . . He will take your daughters to be his perfumers and
cooks and bakers. He will take the best of your fields and vineyards and olive orchards and give them to his courtiers. . . . And
you shall be his slaves" (8:11, 13-14, 17, italics added).

This dire warning has no effect: "But the people refused to
listen to the voice of Samuel; they said, 'No! but we are determined to have a king over us, so that we also may be like other
nations, and that our king may govern us and go out before us
and fight our battles'" (8:19-20). It's pretty clear that, in the
name of national security, they do not listen to the voice of God.

Which raises the question: Were they ever meant to have a
king at all? Backward reading allows us to ask that very intriguing
question. Not out of disregard for God's word. On the contrary,
it's because we begin to cherish and love it, as a murder-mystery,
hidden-code masterpiece that invites *us* into the dialogue, all
for the sake of dismantling our idols, deconstructing our gods,
smashing our little religious games, and imagining *this*—this is
no ordinary account of history. These are the bold and splendid

and shocking seismic markers, cryptic clues, of what happens when a wholly other God leaves it all on the shelf and dives into our world, risking even being misunderstood in ridiculous ways.

Let's return to the prophet Isaiah. At the end of the grand story, Isaiah speaks from the viewpoint of a broken, humiliated, suffering people. Babylon has conquered the so-called chosen ones and has forcibly removed them from the land and taken them to a strange place. It's a hauntingly close parallel to what President Andrew Jackson did to the Cherokee when he drove them to Oklahoma on the Trail of Tears.

Yet in the midst of this unthinkable horror, this separation of the people from their land and their temple, in exile, the prophet Isaiah dares to speak this new thing. Yahweh, God, points to these people, to these humiliated and powerless and broken and suffering ones, and says:

> Here, is my servant, whom I uphold,
>   my chosen, in whom my soul delights;
> I have put my spirit upon him;
>   he will bring forth justice to the nations.
> . . . .
> A bruised reed he will not break,
>   and a dimly burning wick he will not quench;
>   he will faithfully bring forth justice.
> He will not grow faint or be crushed
>   until he has established justice in the earth;
>   and the coastlands wait for his teaching.
> (Isaiah 42:1, 3-4)

The chosen one, the people Israel, is called "my servant" by this God. It's not exactly a new title. It was used during the time of Moses. But the bold, new thing is to find the "servant of Yahweh" language here in the *ruins*. Here, in exile, as a suffering, broken, humiliated people, Israel is reminded of its relation to Yahweh. Taken into captivity, marched on this trail of tears—you'd expect a people that is self-absorbed, grieving the loss of everything: the loss of its temple and, apparently, the loss of its God. But in this great prophetic proclamation, Yahweh, in the blink of an eye, changes the subject, wakes the people up, rattles these dry bones, calls the chosen people out of their grief and misery, and gives them work to do.

What work are they called to? What chosen task is this chosen people to accomplish? In a word, it is the work of *justice*! This chosen people is to "bring forth justice to the nations" (42:1), to "faithfully bring forth justice" (42:3), and to "not grow faint or be crushed until [justice is established] in the earth" (42:4).

This justice has a very particular meaning. It was there in the stories of Moses, and it is taken up here and developed by the prophets. Justice means a reordering of social life and social power so that the weak (such as widows and orphans) may live a life of dignity, security, and well-being. Justice means that the scales are tipped in favor of the vulnerable. Unlike Babylon, who snaps the bent reeds in two and extinguishes the dimly burning wicks, this people is chosen to pursue a different way in the world, the way of justice.

And that is just a taste of how you read the Hebrew Bible backward. Starting with the prophets' critique of the kings and the conquest, you radicalize and universalize this God of liberation. God wills this liberation not simply for these "chosen ones" but precisely *through* these chosen ones. This chosen people becomes the redemptive suffering servant of the world. They are chosen, called to witness to a higher judgment and a higher mercy. They are at the center of the conflict between stubborn human violence and the God of steadfast love, who enters our world in the name of peace and liberation.

Behold this new thing: Israel's chosenness is good news for all people. This is not a zero-sum game. There is not a fixed quantity, a limited stockpile of the steadfast love of Yahweh. The choosing of one does not imply a rejection of the other. In fact, it is just the opposite. In this one, all the peoples are chosen by God.

Israel is a gift to the world. "I have given you as a covenant to the people, a light to the nations" Yahweh says (Isaiah 42:6, NRSV). Israel's chosen-ness is not for itself, but for others.

Behold, a new thing. Chosen-ness doesn't happen all at once. It is not an event that existed at a certain point in time. It is moving. Chosen-ness keeps moving on. Perhaps any kind of exclusion is only temporary and transient. Perhaps any kind of negation will itself be negated in this great chain of choosing.

Behold, a new thing. Suffering, pain, loss, grief—these things are not the marks of rejection but the signs of the odd God who is working to redeem the world. Here we come face-to-face with mystery—the mystery of evil, of created things that rise up and reject the creator, of broken cords of love, of rebellion, greed, self-obsession, and violence. It is the mystery of the disturbance and the disruption of the perfect love with which this odd God tries to love the world. It is the mystery of the Trail of Tears, the mystery of internment camps, the mystery of the Holocaust in which six million suffering servants of Yahweh were shot and hanged and gassed and burned to death.

I cannot tell you that suffering has any meaning, that it makes any sense whatsoever. I am not worthy. But the prophet Isaiah can tell us that the suffering ones can suffer on behalf of others, that in Israel's agony, all peoples are involved, that Israel's suffering is a sacrifice, and that Israel's endurance is a ritual, a meaning to be disclosed to all people in the hour of Israel's redemption, which is still to come. Isaiah dares to speak these words: that Israel's future will not end in despair and abandonment but in deliverance and redemption, and that through Israel's suffering, redemption will come to all. Isaiah dares to speak these words:

> He was despised and rejected by others;
>   a man of suffering and acquainted with infirmity;
> and as one from whom others hide their faces
>   he was despised, and we held him of no account.

Surely he has borne our infirmities
and carried our diseases;
yet we accounted him stricken,
struck down by God, and afflicted.
But he was wounded for our transgressions,
crushed for our iniquities;
upon him was the punishment that made us whole,
and by his bruises we are healed.

. . . .

Out of his anguish he shall see light;
he shall find satisfaction through his knowledge.
The righteous one, my servant, shall make many righteous,
and he shall bear their iniquities.
(Isaiah 53:3-5, 11)

Behold, a new thing. Israel's chosen-ness is bigger than us and our ability to make choices. It's about God, this odd God who keeps trying to choose us. The point of Israel's chosen-ness is to reveal the patience, the passion, the self-giving, the steadfast love of this odd God.

The Hebrew prophets pronounce judgment, but they never pronounce abandonment. This odd God loves with an other-worldly kind of love, a love that is patient, a love that does not seek to destroy but to nurture the other, a love that overcomes the unfaithfulness of the people, a love that forgives their sins, negates their negation, rejects their rejection.

Behold, a new thing. Chosen and called, Israel, the people, can now be *for others.* Their chosen-ness is for others. They are loved with a love that repairs the damage, undoes the violence, overcomes the separation.

Part Two: The Newer Testament and How to Read the Gospels Backward

Now that you've mastered that art of reading the Hebrew Bible backward, I'll turn your attention to the other testament in the Bible. I hope you can put up with a bit of asymmetry here. Because this time we will be treating not the scope of the entire New Testament but simply imagining the possibility that each of the four Gospels (Matthew, Mark, Luke, and John) were written backward, from the perspective of a crucified and risen Christ.

The Backstory: The Enlightenment Embarrassment over the Resurrection

There was a period (in modernity—roughly the last two hundred to four hundred years, depending on which European White Guy you choose as your spokes-model) when Christians were sort of embarrassed about the ending of our Gospels (Matthew, Mark, Luke, and John), sort of embarrassed about the resurrection—the resurrection of Jesus Christ from the dead. For some, it became a nonessential to the faith.

For example, it was absolutely nonessential for a good modernist like Thomas Jefferson. Have you heard of *The Jefferson Bible*, also known as *The Life and Morals of Jesus of Nazareth*?[2] In classic modernist form Jefferson actually took a razor blade and cut out all the bits of the Bible that he deemed too supernatural or too magical, including all of that superstitious, primitive mumbo jumbo about the resurrection. Christians can mock and scorn Jefferson all they want, but he actually did something pretty brave—he took to the limit what we all think from time to time. What is really *in* the Bible? What are the most important parts? Are there parts that are the center, as well as parts that are nonessential? What would *you* cut out of it?

But, please, before you get out your razor blades, let me tell you about some more recent developments. In our context, partly due to our love/hate relationship with modernity, there has been something of a revival. Preachers and theologians are claiming,

---

2. Thomas Jefferson, *The Life and Morals of Jesus of Nazareth* (St. Louis, Chicago, and New York: N.D. Thompson Publishing Company, 1902).

once again, that the resurrection of Jesus from the dead is absolutely essential to the faith, both theologically and historically.

Theologically, the resurrection of Christ is seen not as a trick that God did to wow the people into submission, but rather as part of the unfolding of the Triune God's purposes for the world. The resurrection is a manifestation of the relationship of trust, an outcropping of the self-circulating love that the Father, Son, and Spirit shared before the creation of this world.

But there are also commonsense *historical* reasons why the resurrection is once again being considered essential to the faith. Something happened—something big, something that really did turn the world upside down. There is no other way to account for "the apostolic witness," the early Christian community that rose up and confronted the Roman Empire with the message of care and forgiveness and the big notion (that modernity claimed to have invented but actually stole from Jesus) of the inherent, utterly gifted worth of every human being and all of creation.

At any rate, something happened in the resurrection and the apostolic witness to the resurrection. And the gospels actually make the most sense if we read them backward.[3] Something really happened that allowed for this movement, this resistance to the Roman Empire that took hold in its midst. That something was the resurrection and what we call the apostolic witness to the resurrection—the women and men who devoted their lives to this good news, this story of God with us in this loving, gracious, forgiving, life-changing way.

---

3. Have you ever had the commonsensical notion that "Gee, it's sort of all or nothing, isn't it? If Jesus Christ didn't rise from the dead, then what are we doing here? We might as well be at the Rotary Club, or the bar, or out stimulating the economy with those tax rebates that we haven't even gotten yet." If that thought has crossed your mind, maybe it's because that commonsensical notion is true.

Theologian and biblical scholar James Alison has given us a brilliant backward reading of the gospels.[4] His reading goes something like this: The resurrection of Jesus is God holding up a mirror to our violence and overcoming it with God's forgiveness, justice, and love. In the resurrection/crucifixion, God takes the worst that we can do—the most cruel and violent scapegoating of an innocent victim—and God reveals the heart of our victim-making mechanisms, not in order to condemn us, but in order to forgive and to heal and to show us new, peaceful ways to live together. What the crucified and risen Christ makes known to us is something Alison calls "the intelligence of the victim"—the deep, thick, contextual knowledge of what it means to be victimized, to be wounded and rejected and cast out.[5] All the victims of history, all those who have suffered and died without justice, share this "intelligence of the victim," which is really known only by those who suffer violence, until Jesus comes along and blows everything wide open.[6] Jesus stands with all the victims of history—embraces them, comforts them, holds them up so that we can see our violence, so that this whole big mess might be redeemed and healed, making us all ready for the party at the end of the world.

God as the risen victim, coming back from the dead to confront us and offer us a new start: this stuff is remarkable for both its beauty and its utter realism. It is not sentimental. It acknowledges that we are violent creatures who sometimes only know how to get along by making victims that unify us in our hatred for a common enemy. But it is so hopeful. Because Jesus' resurrection is the undoing of our violence, from the perspective of the victim. In Christ, God *becomes our victim* in order to confront us and call us to other ways of living together.

---

4. James Alison, *Raising Abel: The Recovery of the Eschatological Imagination* (New York: Crossroad, 1996).

5. Ibid., 3.

6. Ibid.

So if you try this backward-reading strategy, here's what you get. This risen-from-the-dead victim, through God's creative grace, illuminates all of the history that came before him. God was working all along to overcome and undo our violence. The intelligence of the victim, the deep, intimate, personal knowledge of the victim, was there all along.

Moving backward, from the resurrection to the crucifixion, to the garden of Gethsemane, through all of Jesus' sometimes puzzling teachings and parables, in the birth stories, in John's bold claims that Jesus was with God before the world was made—everything is illuminated by looking backward from the resurrection, by Jesus' deep, intimate knowledge of God's subversive love, working to undo our violence.

The Preexistence of Christ? Really?

The preexistence of Jesus? What? Like he lived before he was born? Frankly, that sounds pretty kooky. (Talk about something nonessential.)

If you treat it as a little piece of metaphysics or speculation or some doctrine that you are supposed to believe, it really means nothing. What's the point? It is only by going backward from the resurrection that this makes any sense at all.

In the seventeenth chapter of John, we have this very direct and blunt claim of Jesus. He prays, "So now, Father, glorify me in your own presence with the glory that I had in your presence before the world existed" (John 17:5, NRSV). "Ya know, back when we were together, before I was born, in my preexistent state." This only makes sense if you read it backward, from the "risen victim" stuff of the resurrection. But then not only does it make sense, it also becomes sort of mind-blowing, sublime, gorgeous, and intensely pleasurable.

Anyhow, here it is (I'm leaning heavily on James Alison here): Jesus, the risen victim, illuminates things—backward. When God raises Jesus from the dead, God reveals to us that the gracious self-giving of the victim is "identical with" the gracious giving that is the creation. In Jesus' resurrection, looking backward, we can now understand creation, the created world itself, as given in "a relationship of purely gratuitous giving, with no ulterior motives, with no desire for control or domination, but rather a giving-ness which permits creatures to share graciously in the life of the creator."[7]

The intelligence of the victim opened up for the disciples the very structure of the universe. The presence of the crucified-and-risen victim made possible for the disciples a new perception: the perception that grace is prior to all that is, that creation itself flows out of the same grace that lifts up the crucified and forgiving victim. God is the fount of all self-giving, both in taking the form of the victim and, way before that, in creating the universe. Grace is prior to all that is. The gracious self-giving of God into the hands of humans—what John calls the "handing over"—in order to become a human victim is done so that humans can learn to quit killing each other and come to participate in a new way of living. This, according to Alison, is "the true perspective on creation, revealed by the intelligence of the victim."[8] The risen victim, "by revealing the purpose or finality of the whole act, also simultaneously reveals the dynamic behind its beginning."[9]

Again, we move backward: the innocent victim, God handed over, is risen from the dead, and humans are handed over into this mysterious, blessed discovery. This discovery "begins with the blood of the cross, and moves backwards until it comes to be understood that the crucified-and-risen Lord reveals the full sense of creation"[10]—the radical self-giving love that brings all things into being.

---

7. James Alison, *The Joy of Being Wrong* (New York: Crossroad, 1998), 94.
8. Ibid., 98.
9. Ibid.
10. Ibid., 99.

So what? In God's love, all things live and move and have their being. The same passionate, creative, ridiculous, bold, bleeding love that came here and got so deeply involved with our violence and raised Jesus from the dead—that is the exact character of love that lies at the heart of all of creation!

So what? We have a new foundation. A foundation that undoes all our foundations. A foundation of radical, suffering love that lies at the heart of every atom, every proton and neutron, every particle, every wave, every breath. The violence is ours. It is real. And we don't need a religion of sentiment and cheer and do-goodiness that takes us out of all the suffering. What we need is what we could never have imagined that we needed. What we need comes to us from out of the blue. Jesus Christ, the victim of our violence, comes back from the dead. Horrifying, perhaps, at first, yet we finally will all discover that he comes not to condemn but to forgive.

Part Three: Handy Tips for Reading the Bible

What if you could bring your honesty, your questions, your imaginations to reading and interpreting the Bible? My hope is that you will see the big picture—namely liberation, a justice that is rooted in God's grace. And yet still you will be able to wrestle with the details—the record of a gracious God and a resistant, idolatrous, stubborn humanity that is still figuring it out. In the freedom and adventurous grace I will close out this chapter with a short list of tips for reading the Bible.

1. Don't read the Bible alone. Sign up for a smart, critical-thinking Bible study at a local church.

2. Get a good plausibility helper (a smart but plainly written commentary). Look, if you're reading this book, you've probably got this virus called "critical thinking." You've been infected. When you sit down to read the Bible, why should you expect to suddenly put all that on the shelf, shut your brain off, and read with some sort of magical

gift of unquestioning faith? What a good commentary will do, at least, is help you understand the document you're reading—its context, how it was composed, what kind of symbols and images are being employed, what sort of cultural forms it's messing with—all these things that will make you say, "Oh, that makes sense. That's plausible." And then, hopefully, just when you've made it all plausible, that's when the Holy Spirit will come and knock it all down again, expose you to yourself, and show you something you really couldn't have told yourself.

3. Read it backward, especially the Hebrew Bible. Read the prophets—Isaiah, Jeremiah, and the others. Note what they say about justice and peace and Israel being a light to the nations of the world. Note their radical extension of the liberation that was begun in the event of Israel's exodus out of slavery in Egypt. And then, with their critique ringing in your ears, go back and read the conquest books. What you'll find is sarcasm, irony, and plot twists and turns—all in all a rich, critical dialogue that raises deep questions about a people slow to learn the steadfast love of this God (just as we are slow to learn that steadfast love).

4. Remember the *living* word. I think the Protestant Reformers had it right on this one. The Bible itself is *not* the Word of God. Rather, it is supposed to be the *witness* to the *living Word*. For Christians, the living Word is Jesus, the Christ, and our knowledge of his love through the Holy Spirit. For Jews as well, the scriptures are not dead. They are the wondrous record of a God of justice and mercy, a God of steadfast love, who is remembered in the worshipping community.

Please remember. The Bible is not the word. The Bible is a witness, an authoritative witness to the ways and works of the living God, who cannot be captured in propositions and arguments.

10

The Seven Deadly Myths about Sin, or How to Sin like a Christian

In case you haven't noticed, there's this little three-letter word, a highly religious word, that some pastors and theologians often avoid. It's a word that has to do, roughly, with transgression, waywardness, distortion, missing the mark, erring, indiscretion, the shadow side. That three-letter word we so love to avoid? S-I-N. Sin. There. I said it. And I feel better.

But let me explain. Some of you might think that those of us who are careful about using this word simply don't believe in sin, that we avoid talking about sin because we consider it irrelevant, uncouth, tasteless—an antiquated notion that we have evolved beyond. Quite to the contrary, some of us are such experts on sin that we don't even know how to talk about it.

Believe it or not, many contemporary pastors and theologians often avoid this word because it triggers all the shame and guilt and moralism of the folk religion that is so contrary to what the Bible really says. So we look for ways to talk about sin without using that word—using other words, images, and stories that name the violence, apathy, and darkness that inhabit the human heart. But this chapter will change all of that. Instead of avoiding the word *sin* and trying to reconfigure it, what if we get right after it? What if, instead of using new words and images, we try to redeem (to restore the meaning of) this old word?

Introducing: The Magnificent Seven

Who will rescue us from these dangerous, denigrating, shame inducing distortions about sin? Thankfully, I am not on my own here. I'm calling in some hired hands, some creative and imaginative theologians and cultural critics who I'm enlisting to shoot down these myths.

Do you know the film *The Magnificent Seven?* The John Sturges existentialist-Western remake of Kurasawa's *The Seven Samuari*, in which a band of oppressed Mexican peasant villagers hire seven gunfighters to help defend their homes? One by one, the viewer is introduced to these absolutely ultra-cool hired guns who smoke thin cigars and are played by the likes of Yul Brenner, Steve McQueen, James Coburn, and Charles Bronson.

Well, in this, my chapter on sin, we have some hired guns of our own, to help us debunk and dispel these myths about sin. Think of them as The Magnificent Seven of Misconduct, The Seven Samauri of Sin. And so, for your edification, I hereby present "The Seven Deadly Myths about Sin."

Myth #1: You Were Born a Sinner

One of the strangest developments in the history of sin is the doctrine of original sin. We attribute this view to Augustine, the beloved and brilliant bishop of Hippo, born in the mid fourth century.

Here's what seems to have gone wrong in Augustine's view that sin is inherited at birth. In Romans 5:12, Paul writes that "death spread to all persons because all persons sinned." Augustine, working from a Latin translation of the New Testament (something called the Vulgate), took Romans 5 to mean that because of Adam, death spread to all people. Therefore, at birth, human beings are all already guilty, already depraved.

By the late Middle Ages, the official teaching of the church was more or less Augustinian: the church subscribed to original sin and endorsed infant baptism as the remedy. Baptizing an infant was believed to remove the stain, the curse, with which humans enter the world. When the Reformers (both Protestant and Catholic) failed to really examine Augustine's formulation, the modern church was left with a view of original sin that was not necessarily what the Bible means to say about sin—a view that is now ridiculed by ridiculers and scoffed at by scoffers.

ıllıllıllıllı

The first of our magnificent seven is the late, great James William McClendon Jr. McClendon, a theologian—a Southern Baptist theologian no less—studied the history of the doctrine of original sin all his life. And according to gunslinger McClendon, in this very important text from Romans, Paul was talking about a puzzle, a paradox, a riddle wrapped in an enigma: "Death spread to all persons . . . because all persons sinned" (Romans 5:12). Paul is not making a point about Adam transferring sin to us. Paul is lamenting, wailing, grieving: the dominion of death, the death world.

Paul is not trying to get us out of our responsibility for sin, as if we could blame it all on Adam. Quite to the contrary, Paul is contrasting *our world* of sin and death with something else, something I'll tell you about later. But for now, back to the myths.

Myth 2: Your Body Is Sinful

The idea of the body being sinful is a myth that we can also blame on the doctrine of original sin mashed up with some badly interpreted Greek philosophy. This myth is based on a dualism of mind over body, spirit over matter.

A guiding narrative for this myth is Plato's metaphor of the human spirit as a fresh, clear, pure flowing river. Unfortunately, as it flows down the mountainside of the world, it picks up all manner of dirt and silt and muck. Your mind/soul/spirit is pure. The world, creation/stuff/matter, is tainted and dirty.

What you end up with is this nasty little dualism. The *real* you, the spirit you, is pure. It's your body that is holding you back. Your body, your flesh, is tainted, and dirty. It must be pummeled and subdued in order for your higher nature, your spirit, to be liberated.

Alas, in this paradigm, how seamlessly our body becomes a metaphor for the created world: the body of the earth is just like your own body. At worst, it is the place of darkness and sin. Even at best, the created world is nothing but an elaborate stage on which to play out the winning or losing of your salvation.

Who will protect us from this myth?

ıııııııııııı

Please allow me to introduce to you one of my favorite professors of theology: Rosemary Radford Ruether. She has some very important words for you.

"Whatever it is, sin," according to Ruether, "is not pure spirit succumbing to dirty matter."[1] Sin is not about carnal, earthbound urges that corrupt our pure soul. Rather, insidiously, we sin in part by trying to blame "the flesh" for sins that start within our own hearts and minds. And even insidiouslier, we sin when we disrupt and distort the created order—when we create dysfunc-

---

1. Rosemary Radford Ruether, *Liberation Theology: Human Hope Confronts Christian History and American Power* (New York: Paulist Press, 1972), 12.

tional relationships with the earth, with our ecological community, and with each other—and we preserve these dysfunctional relationships in social codes.

It takes a body to sin. But don't blame sin on your body. Blaming the body (blaming Eve?) is one of the oldest tricks in the book (of sin).

Myth 3: Sex Is Sinful

One more myth that is reinforced by the doctrine of original sin says that sexuality itself is somehow inherently tainted, sinful, and dirty. Augustine not only blamed Adam for the sin we inherit (that original-sin stuff), he also believed that the very act of procreation was the means by which original sin was transmitted.

And when you suggest to people that something as powerful and intimate as sex could be the source of this original sin that we pass on to each other, you are playing with fire. From the Middle Ages through the Victorian era and down to the present day, this notion that sex is dirty has cast a very strange and curious shadow over human sexuality. The result: we splinter off acts of sex from the relationship between intimates, and we make those acts taboo and fetishize them. That which is playful and beautiful and creative becomes deviant.

||||||||||||||

Riding over the eastern horizon, from his home in London, comes the Clint Eastwood of academia, our next hired gun: James Alison. What Alison suggests is that when you equate sex with sin, you suddenly have no ethic of sex. All sex becomes bad sex! So there's no such thing as good sex and bad sex, good love and bad love. There's no (in the words of Alison) "discerning when love is love for another person and when it is self-love using the other as a mirror." Then "there's no difference between love and jealousy, between possessiveness and a passion for the growth and well-being of another."[2]

But imagine that sex is not inherently sinful, that sex is something like the creative expression of shared intimacy and pleasure between two lovers who deeply trust each other, who have pledged a love for each other that is beyond changing conditions. Then sexuality is not inherently evil and tainted. Then it is "not intrinsically . . . but only accidentally perverse." The result is that there can be good and bad sex, mutual relationships and manipulative ones. And, contrary to this myth that sex is inherently sinful, "what is good and what is bad can be worked out."[3]

Myth 4: Boys Know All about Sin, and They Need Not Listen to Girls

Have you ever noticed that, for most of church history, theologians, priests, and all the other official teachers of doctrine have been male? Is it plausible to imagine that this might have some impact on our inherited beliefs and definitions of sin?

ıııııııııııı

Riding into town all the way from the 1960s, the brave and bold pioneering days of feminist thought, comes our next debunker, Valerie Saiving, who helped the whole world of contemporary theology think perspectivally about sin (which is a fancy way of saying that your social, economic, racial, and gendered outlook on the world shapes your definition of sin).

"The temptations of woman *as woman* are not the same as the temptations of man *as man*," according to Saiving.[4] And the

---

2. James Alison, *Faith beyond Resentment: Fragments Catholic and Gay* (New York: Crossroad, 2001), 138–39.

3. Ibid., 139–40.

4. Valerie Saiving, "The Human Situation: A Feminine View," in *Womanspirit Rising: A Feminist Reader in Religion*, ed. Carol P. Christ & Judith Plaskow (New

specifically feminine forms of sin have a quality that can never be encompassed by such terms as *pride* and *will to power*. "They are better suggested by such items as triviality, distractibility, and diffuseness; lack of an organizing center or focus; dependence on others for one's own self-definition."[5] In short, according to Saiving, the temptations of women are centered around the "underdevelopment or negation of the self."[6]

Even if you can't get with her language and her analysis, Saiving does bring something indispensable to the table. No longer can we let one perspective on the world (especially the dominant one) articulate what sin is. We must listen to voices of the other, especially the voices from the underside of history, those who might have a completely different perspective on just what is wrong with the world.

Myth 5: Sin Is Committed by Individual Persons

The next myth views us all as individual, separate atoms. This makes sin a matter of personal decision, will, and action. It's as if what we do does not affect others, as if there is no great web of relationship, as if each one of us is an island.

⠀⠀⠀⠀⠀⠀⠀||||||||||||

Now appearing in our chapter is a truly imposing figure. As hip as Yul Brynner, as cool as Steve McQueen, and smarter than both of them put together, it's El-Hajj Malik El-Shabazz, aka Malcom X.

Are there social institutions that are sinful, even demonic? Reformist theologians from the early twentieth century, like Walter Rauschenbusch, tried to say there is something inexplicably evil, truly sinful, about the way social institutions are capable of

---

York: HarperCollins, 1979, 1992), 37.
5. Ibid.
6. Ibid.

perpetuating poverty. Malcom X applied these same intuitions to the dual structures of economic exploitation and racism. According to Malcom, sin, evil, the demonic masks itself in social structures that are bigger than you and me, that take on a life of their own and operate as systems of which individual subjects are not even aware.[7]

You must read chapter 1 of Malcom's autobiography. That's an order. In this chapter, Malcom so graphically describes how his family was unraveled by systemic structures of "charitable institutions" that masked an inherent racism:

> I truly believe that if ever a state social agency destroyed a family, it destroyed ours. We wanted and tried to stay together. Our home didn't have to be destroyed. But the Welfare, the courts, and their doctor, gave us the one-two-three punch. . . .
>
> I knew I wouldn't be back to see my mother again because it could make me a very vicious and dangerous person—knowing how they had looked at us as numbers and as a case in their book, not as human beings. And knowing that my mother in there was a statistic that didn't have to be, that existed because of a society's failure, hypocrisy, greed, and lack of mercy and compassion. Hence I have no mercy or compassion in me for a society that will crush people, and then penalize them for not being able to stand up under the weight.[8]

I'm convinced that Malcom's rant is not far from the Apostle Paul's notion of "principalities and powers" in Ephesians 3, in which Paul suggests that humanity is not made up of unconnected individuals, but rather these corporate structures that

---

7. Malcom X with Alex Haley, *The Autobiography of Malcom X* (New York: Grove, 1965).
8. Ibid., 22.

mask our collective evil: kingdoms, empires, institutions, corporations, and maybe even churches. Paul's doctrine of principalities and powers suggests that these structures have an uncanny power to get ahold of us and radically distort our collective vision.

Myth 6: Sin Is "Out There"; We Are (Personally) Innocent

If myth 5 ignores social institutions and the effects of sinful environments, defeating this myth will call us back, once again, to personal responsibility. The sixth myth says that sin is the result of our entanglements with the world, outside influences without which we would more or less be pure. What if we could only rid ourselves of our muddy, dirty environment? What if we could just start over and leave this polluted place behind?

This is the proud American myth about sin, the myth grounded in the vision of America as *The New Eden*. It assumes that we can simply move away, start over. That by starting over in a new land, we can strip ourselves of all those old, worn-out, and corrupt influences that held us back.

⸻⸻⸻

For the debunking of this myth, we turn to the world of literature, to one of the great critics of American idealism, Nathaniel Hawthorne, and his obscure but brilliant short story "Earth's Holocaust."[9]

"Once upon a time," Hawthorne begins, "this wide world had become so overburdened with an accumulation of worn-out trumpery, that the inhabitants determined to rid themselves of it

---

9. Nathaniel Hawthorne, "Earth's Holocaust," in *Moses from an Old Manse* (New York: Thomas Y. Crowell, 1900), 154–79.

by a general bonfire."[10] These weary pioneers build a great, purging bonfire fueled by all the artifacts of the oppressive *old world*—things like badges of knighthood, patents of nobility, the purple robes of royalty, the crowns, globes, and scepters of emperors and kings. As the fire grows, they round up all the liquor and wine, all the boxes of tea and bags of coffee in the world, all the tobacco, all of the fashionable clothing that so captivates the consumers. They toss in all of their cannons, guns, swords, and other weapons. They throw in books and pamphlets: works of philosophy, literature, history. Last, but not least, they throw in all the symbols and sources of religion: all the crosses, fonts, sacramental vessels, as well as every prayer book and Bible that can be found.

But just as this great, purging fire is consuming every last vestige of the old world, a *critic* appears, with the last word: "There is one thing which you have forgotten to throw into the fire," he says, "the human heart itself!" He ends with this warning: "And, unless they hit upon some method of purifying that foul cavern, forth from it will re-issue all the shapes of wrong and misery—the same old shapes, or worse ones. . . . Oh, take my word for it, it will be the old world yet."[11]

Beware the myth of innocence, the myth of the New Eden.

Myth 7: We Can All Know What Sin Is by Simply Looking Within

Let's get to it. In our context, the big lie is this folk religion, this *Ameri-religianity* that is filling the void as particular religious practice declines. This folk religion identifies sin and limits it to "being naughty": lying, stealing, cheating, adultery. According to this folk religion, these are the bad deeds that will send us to hell, if our good deeds do not outweigh our bad deeds. Behind this

10. Ibid., 154.
11. Ibid., 179.

folk religion is the assumption that we can have clear and direct knowledge of the naughty things we do by "looking deep within," by taking a personal moral inventory.

This folk religion, "Ameri-religianity," places its faith in the power of "the conscience" in which Jiminy Cricket is high priest, teaching little children to "always let your conscience be your guide," and then hanging around as a little conscience-reinforcing figure perched on our shoulder: "Give a little whistle and always let your conscience be your guide." The big assumption here is that we have some natural and innate knowledge of good and bad, as if we can simply hold up a mirror to ourselves and see our sins.

|||||||||||||

Who can we hire as a mercenary against this myth of "conscience"?

For my money, there's not a better shot than one Karl Barth, the Pride of Basel, Switzerland. Here he is, weighing in at a strapping 154 pounds, smoking some really strong tobacco, wearing thick little spectacles, and speaking in a hardly intelligible Swiss-German accent.

You're standing there, looking in the mirror, scrutinizing yourself for all your faults, flaws, blemishes, stains, and sins. And Karl Barth draws his gun, takes aim, and *shoots the mirror right out of your hand.*

You can't know about sin from looking in the mirror, he tells you. You can only know what sin is by looking at Christ. "Christian sin" is just that, sin against Christ, against this perfect relationship of trust that inheres in the Trinity.

Sin has to do with relationship. It is, at its core, a violation of relationship, a violation of trust. Sin is not simply the naughty things you do, like the seven deadly sins of wrath, greed, sloth, pride, lust, envy, and gluttony (although it certainly can include those things). No. Sin is the darkness that the light illumines.

So, ultimately, sin can be properly and truly known only as it is forgiven.

Our hired gun has written these gems:[12]

- "Sin may be known in its nature, reality, implications and consequences as it is opposed, vanquished and done away with by Jesus Christ."
- "The Christian concept of sin is not to be gained in a vacuum, *remoto Christo*, but from the Gospel, the good news of [humanity's] liberation by and for the free God."
- "In all its forms sin is [humanity's] perverted dealing with the stern goodness and righteous mercy of God."
- As enmity against God, sin is "unmasked, discovered and judged as [humanity] is confronted by the Gospel, by the living Jesus Christ in the Gospel."

Whatever "conscience" might be, it is not a biblical concept. The Bible does not teach us that we can simply look in a mirror and see our naughty deeds, our "sin." Sin can't really be defined by looking within. It can't be defined independently of the God who truly loves us.

So how do you "sin like a Christian"? Sin is sin against God. It is not simply a breaking of the law. It is relational. It is against God and God's love, and not against a set of rules or a certain cultural morality.

According to John the Evangelist, through Jesus, the Word made flesh, "the light shines in the darkness" (John 1:5). This light casts a shadow as serious as a heart attack. Our sin, in all the mysterious and devious ways it tries to mask itself, is part of the death world. It will be judged.

But the last word is the best. Our judge is our redeemer. Our darkness is illuminated by the light.

---

12. Karl Barth, *Church Dogmatics*, vol. 4, *The Doctrine of Reconciliation, Part Three, First Half* (Edinburgh: T&T Clark, 1961), 369f.

||||||||||||

I've grown very fond of our magnificent seven: Jim McClendon, Rosemary Radford Ruether, James Alison, Valerie Saiving, Malcom X, Nathaniel Hawthorne, and Karl Barth. An unlikely group of prophets and friends, they could have my back in any theological gunfight. But in the end, this is only theology. The real stuff happens in Word and Sacrament: when we hear the Word of grace and gather around the table with our fellow sinners and saints who remember this Christ in the breaking of the bread.

11

The Hell Chapter

On Heaven, Hell, and the Last Judgment: The Second Voyage of Saint Brendan

Hᴀᴠᴇ ʏᴏᴜ ʜᴇᴀʀᴅ ᴏꜰ Saint Brendan—the saint from County Kerry, in Ireland—and his voyage? I was doing some research on the subject of heaven, hell, and the last judgment, and I came across these writings: *The Voyage of St. Brendan*, otherwise known as *The Navagatio.*

Born in 486 ᴄ.ᴇ., Brendan was intrigued by tales of the afterlife—specifically by tales of "a land promised to the saints." He became obsessed with a singular vision, to see if he could find that land, this side of the grave. And so he built a coracle of wattle (a frame made from twigs), covered it with hides tanned in oak bark softened with butter, set up a mast and a sail, and after a prayer upon the shore, embarked on a seven-year seafaring journey.

Brendan never reached his destination. He was able to glimpse the "land promised to the saints" but was hindered from entering by a great river guarding its entrance. However, along the way, his journey took him to such exotic places as Sheep Island, The Paradise of Birds, and the Islet of Paul the Hermit. He met many fantastic creatures: Jasconius the Friendly Whale, upon whose back Brendan celebrated Easter; "a predatory sea-cat, as big as a horse"; and a holy hound that guided his crew to safety. And, of course, Brendan also sailed past the edge of hell. Past Fiery Island, the Island of Smiths, and the Island of Small Dark Fiends, while giant demons hurled great lumps of burning slag at Brendan and his crew.

I've got one word for ya: sequel!

That's right. We're bringing back Saint Brendan. Fifteen hundred years after his original voyage, he's going to lead us on our own journey through heaven, hell, and the last judgment— or, more precisely, a voyage through some commonly held views of heaven, hell, and the last judgment. Who better than Saint Brendan, the explorer, to guide us on our trip into the afterlife? If it works, I'm going to write some songs and turn it into a musical: "The Second Voyage of Saint Brendan," starring Sean Connery as Saint Brendan.

And so, dear reader, prepare the coracle of wattle, tan the hides in oak bark softened with butter, and raise the sail.[1]

The Vast Continent of Mediocrity and Shopping

After several days' journey, out on the high seas, we reach our first stop: the Vast Continent of Mediocrity and Shopping. As it turns out, it's a land very much like our own.

Here's what most of the natives think about heaven and hell. People are either mostly good or mostly bad. If the good you do

---

1. This chapter leans heavily on the work of Douglas John Hall and his brilliant analysis of a North American folk religion based on heaven and hell. You can find a much more detailed account of these matters in *Confessing the Faith: Christian Theology in a North American Context* (Minneapolis: Fortress Press, 1996), 513–18.

outweighs the bad, you will go to heaven. On the flip side, if you do more bad things than good, you will go to hell. What's really strange about the Vast Continent of Mediocrity and Shopping? Long after the natives have lost touch with religion in particular, the inhabitants still cling to this heaven-or-hell folk religion, this notion of immortality, and the moral calculus that undergirds it. You are either good or bad. "Heaven's rewards" and "hell's punishments" thus play a huge role in their folk religion and their morality.[2] What's more, these people are strangely fixated on ancient ideas of heaven and hell—ideas they got, not from their sacred texts, but from the imaginative tales of their culture's middle ages.

Saint Brendan was deeply disturbed by the beliefs of these natives. "Responsible Christians must loudly protest this heaven-and-hell folk religion!" he cried out. "These are *not* simply the doings of innocent, uneducated people. This is a dangerous folk religion, which often calls itself 'Christian' but is, at its core, downright satanic. After all, hell works better when it's subtle." (That was was one of his favorite sayings.)

I could not get him to shut up. It got kind of embarrassing.

"Undergirding this folk mythology lie assumptions about God, humanity, salvation, and ethics that are simply *not Christian*," he said. "This is a folk religion whose beliefs about salvation ignore Jesus Christ and cast him in a false light."[3]

"And one more thing," he continued to rant, "this folk religion of heaven or hell assumes that human good and human evil are easily distinguished and easily separated. It assumes that some are pure and others tainted, that some are light and others are dark. It ignores the complex and thoroughly biblical theme that human beings are a mysterious admixture of good *and* evil, saint *and* sinner, sheep *and* goat."[4]

---

2. Ibid., 513.
3. Ibid.
4. Ibid., 513f.

As we set sail and departed, he continued shouting at the befuddled natives on the shore of the Vast Continent of Mediocrity and Shopping: "No human being is unambiguously on one or the other side of divine judgment. Even the saint remains a sinner and needs forgiveness, and even the sinner is a saint insofar as he or she stands under the divine forgiveness. A pox upon your heaven-or-hell folk religion!"[5] And even though I had no idea what a pox was, I knew he meant it.

The Island of the Evangelicals

A couple of days at sea calmed him down a bit. But just as I was wondering what I had gotten myself into, we spied an island on the horizon. It was smaller than the Vast Continent of Mediocrity and Shopping, but a large island nevertheless. We soon set foot on the Island of the Evangelicals.

The people of the island were not afraid to talk about the afterlife, especially about hell, and in much more specific terms than on the Vast Continent. They talked about the last judgment in the Gospel of Matthew and the Bible's clear teachings of a literal hell into which the evil ones are cast.

According to the Evangelicals we spoke with, there were exactly three alternatives regarding what we are to believe about the afterlife: (1) New Age beliefs, regarding Karma and reincarnation, which are of the kingdom of Satan; (2) universalism, which is the mark of a theological liberalism that denies the truths of Scripture; and (3) the biblically correct belief in a literal hell of physical and psychological torment.

We did note, however, a controversy that was raging. Their big question: Is the punishment everlasting or not? The "Traditionalists" believed in eternal suffering and torment, everlasting conscious punishment, while the "Annihilationists" believed

---

5. Ibid., 514.

that hell would eventually snuff out the lives of the punished. It seems that in 1988, theologian John Stott shocked the Evangelical Island by coming out, as it were, declaring that he himself had Annihilationist leanings.

Saint Brendan took a keen interest in these Evangelicals. He admired their zeal, the passionate way they read the Bible, and the way their faith was a living, daily reality. But he humbly confessed that after scouring all the hell texts in Scripture, he was always impressed that in each text there were limits.

"Look for the limits, Laddie," he told me, cryptically. And so I asked him, "What about Jesus' clear teaching in Matthew about the sheep and the goats? It seems pretty cut-and-dried. Where are the limits in that?"

The Floating Enclave of the Liberals

But before he could answer, we spotted a very strange sight floating by the island. So we jumped in our coracle of wattle and sailed out to explore. We were straightaway invited onboard the Floating Enclave of the Liberals.

Sailing from the left coast of the Vast Continent was a great flotilla of what appeared to be ships but upon further inspection turned out to be old churches, mostly empty, turned upside down and lashed together with the vestments of ex–clergy members.

The boat-churches were nearly empty. But the few people inside—who were still there after so many others had left—were soooooo *nice*. In fact, we walked right into a Sunday-morning church service and were greeted, almost smothered, with warm smiles by the twenty-five or thirty people in attendance, who handed us colorful balloons while a very nice large white woman with a big smile was playing the piano and leading the congregation in singing John Lennon's "Imagine."

These were nice people, who believed in a nice God, a God too nice to bring judgment. Some of them believed that people are inherently good—that the bad things we do are capable of reform, given the proper moral instruction. Others simply believed in the niceness of God.

I looked over at Brendan and tried to anticipate his response, hoping that he'd at least be polite to these nice people. He looked uncomfortable, and I sensed he was about to go into rant mode, when we were again interrupted by a new discovery.

Saint Mary Margaret of the Blessed Sacrament Floating Catholic School

Out on the southeastern horizon, we spotted what appeared to be a barge. We immediately overtook it and were welcomed on board. "Greetings, Romanists!" Saint Brendan bellowed.

And then we both realized we had boarded Saint Mary Margaret of the Blessed Sacrament Floating Catholic School, complete with a very bright sister who was teaching her students about purgatory.

She was young and pretty, with fair, freckled skin and coal-black hair. And she spoke with such eloquence. She was nothing like the nuns I had heard about from my Catholic-school friends. And what she said almost made sense to me. Of course, in talking it over with Saint Brendan, I was quick to shoot down the notion of purgatory, even to make fun of it. I mean, I know that belief in purgatory is not really biblical, and it has led to so much abuse by those in power.

Saint Brendan's response was wise and judicious. He said, "Before you reject any possibility of an intermediate state between heaven and hell, consider this: First of all, purgatory softens that dichotomy of heaven and hell. Compared with a stark heaven and hell, in which we are locked up forever, purgatory seems more compassionate. So in spite of its unbiblical character, it seems more in line with the Bible's picture of a compassionate God."[6]

---

6. Ibid.

"Furthermore," he continued, "some sort of *purging* seems necessary for us to be in the presence of God, does it not? What if there is a holy kind of purging that's not destructive or punitive but truly redemptive? Aren't there things in your present life (greed, envy, lust, sloth, self-aggrandizement, self-loathing) that you would like to have purged away?"[7]

"And finally," he concluded "if we look at the second coming of Christ and the last judgment not simply as static but as dynamic in nature, doesn't it make sense that the final consummation of all things will be a process? Who says there can't be some intermediate state?"

Purgatory? I still don't buy it. But Brendan showed me that maybe there is room for a little humble agnosticism regarding the possibility of an intermediate state.

The Graveyard of the Innocents

We left Saint Mary Margaret of the Blessed Sacrament Floating Catholic School the next day, continuing our expedition. On the morning of the third day there was a sudden change in the air. The conditions turned so cold and gray. Through the fog, we began to notice what appeared to be a vast flow of driftwood bobbing up and down in the water. Upon closer inspection, we recognized that these were in fact tombs, caskets, and sarcophagi.

Brendan told me that we were passing through the Graveyard of the Innocents—floating, drifting tombs with no markers and no one to remember the victims. These were the victims of history. Victims of violence—the murdered, the slain, those slaughtered, beaten, and starved to death in the name of greed, progress, war, racism, homophobia, hatred, and "ethnic cleansing."

And Brendan and I, at the same moment, caught a glimpse of something we had hitherto all but completely ignored. Brendan articulated it with great clarity: "The world is full of

---

7. Ibid.

violence—unspeakable, atrocious violence with real victims, some who are forgotten forever, or so it seems. Isn't our longing for an otherworldly justice entirely appropriate in the face of such monstrous, unfathomable violence?"[8]

He continued, "I understand that your learned psychotherapists consider the belief in immortality an infantile form of wish fulfillment. But in the face of the mystery of violence, isn't the longing for justice an almost logical counterpart? What monsters would we be if we did not demand some sort of accounting for the mystery of innocent suffering? In other words, there is a sense in which 'heaven' is not simply an infantile denial of death by spoiled children. In fact, some sort of after-life judgment seems totally unselfish and other-centered. People ought to be answerable for their treatment of each other and their treatment of the creation. Is this a social presupposition that is necessary for relationship itself? And isn't this belief in an ultimate accounting necessary to sustain our this-worldly visions of justice?"[9]

The Land Promised to the Saints

As I pondered his words, a storm came up and swiftly transported us away in a westerly direction. The strong winds carried us for days. Days passed into weeks.

We were growing tired of our journey when we spied land. Not just land. Saint Brendan recognized it from his journey fifteen hundred years ago: the Land Promised to the Saints, our ultimate destination. Here we would receive all the answers, once and forever and finally.

"You know you can't go in there." Brendan broke it to me gently.

"Why not?" I asked.

"It's guarded by the river, the borders between the living and the dead."

---

8. Ibid., 516.
9. Ibid.

"But this is a sequel," I pleaded. "Something's gotta happen!"
"Mark," he shook his head, "something *is* going to happen. I
am going to go in. And I'm afraid you are going to have to leave
me here. My journey has come to an end."
"No! I won't let you go in there alone," I pleaded.
"Please understand, Mark. It's time," is all he said.
After a few tear-filled moments, I got up the nerve to ask
him. I mean, I came all this way. I wanted to find out something.
So I implored, "Brendan, before you go, please tell me what you
think lies beyond that river—heaven, hell, the last judgment?
What do *you* believe?"
"I want you to decide for yourself," he said. "Explore. Go on
that voyage. Read the Bible, especially the Gospels. Decide for
yourself what it really says about judgment and hell."
"But the Evangelicals study their Bibles. And they come
down on the side of everlasting conscious punishment."
"Ah! That's because they read the Bible in the service of the
tradition of British and American revivalism. Revivalism needs
a literal, terrifying hell, to push the would-be converts to the
moment of decision. Want to test my hypothesis? Just ask an
Evangelical to imagine a conversion experience not based, at
least partially, on the fear of hell. 'No hell? No evangelism,' they
will tell you."
"Well, how do *you* read the Bible?" I asked him.
"Let's stick to the Matthew passage, for now, agreed? Note,
first of all, that this whole story of the sheep and the goats is
apocalyptic literature, a kind of code language for persecuted
people. It gives them hope, helps them to persevere. Note also
that this text is a warning to the self-righteous, a destructive
'goat people' who *think* they are a righteous 'sheep people.' It's
not just that they're not ready for the day of judgment. Rather,
they are totally and completely lost. They think they are something they're not."
He continued, "There's a blessed and holy decentering that
takes place, a prophetic exposing of our idolatry, our ever-present

urge to think of ourselves as something we're not. This is not just 'Get ready.' It's more like 'What if everything you know is wrong? You don't just need to make a little correction here or there. You need to die—and to be born again.'

"The good news of this gospel story is that God *confronts* our idols, our delusions, decenters us, scrambles our idolatrous notions of who is good and who is bad, who is in and who is out. The people *think* they know where to find God. But Christ is hidden in the poor, the sick, the hungry, the naked, the stranger. Matthew is trying to teach us where to look for the kingdom."

"But what about hell?" I asked him. "Do you believe in a literal hell, with real physical and psychological torment?"

He paused for a moment or two and then finally answered. "All right, I'll say a few things. But I still want you to judge for yourself.[10]

"Let me begin by saying this: I don't know. And I don't know if we are supposed to know. Deciding who is in and who is out has proven to be pretty dangerous.

"Second, Jesus has been to hell. He descended into Hades, according to the creed. I don't know what he did. But is it wrong to at least *hope* that hell will be empty? Why should we not will the salvation of all?

"Third, though I have nothing to stand on except the mercy of God, I believe that God's grace has outrun my rebellion, and I believe that God's grace will continue to outrun my rebellion. How can I deny this hope to others?

"Finally, try this. Try shifting the discussion. What if it's not about me? What if it's about God? The question of hell ought to be a question about God and about God's grace. It's not about the sum total of our good or bad deeds. It's about whether God's love

---

10. St. Brendan's words here are a paraphrase of Karl Barth's meditation on the doctrine of *apokatastasis* (the reconciliation of all things) as found in his *Church Dogmatics: The Doctrine of God, Second Half Volume*, vol. 2 (Edinburgh: T. & T. Clark, 1957), 417–19.

will be able to break down our attempts to separate ourselves from God."

"And so, with fear and trembling, I have come to this conclusion: I believe the question of who will be in hell is a question of whether humans will ultimately be able to resist and outrun God's grace, to maintain their isolation from God."

"So how are we to live, in this world?" I asked him. "Should we be afraid of the last judgment? Or should we simply ignore it?"

"Well," he answered, "We must remember that the cross is a place of judgment, not only upon our evil, but also upon our apparent goodness. If we have a destiny that transcends this life, it is the destiny of another, Jesus the Christ, into which, by sheer grace, we have been taken up. I believe we are to live dialectically," he continued. "We hope that our decisions, acts, and judgments reflect God's goodness. But at the same time, we realize that our attempts will always distort God's perfect love."

"And what about the last judgment?" I pressed him.

He replied, "The whole point of the last judgment is not death, but life. It is the victory of the divine righteousness that is to become the foundation for the new creation of all things. The judgment is real. The perfecting of the kingdom includes the ending of injustice. But whatever may come, we must remember *who* this judge is: namely the one who gave himself up for sinners and who suffered the pains and sicknesses of men and women."

||||||||||||

Before we said good-bye and I left him at the gate, Saint Brendan graciously offered me a few more words, words that have become a treasured benediction to me. I call it Saint Brendan's Second Blessing: "Take this judgment seriously. But remember *who* the judge is. Maintain a certain modest reserve—and expect to be surprised. For the one who judges is the crucified one."

12

Toward an Ethics of Butt-Kickin' Grace

I DO NOT TAKE LIGHTLY the title to this chapter. I mean it. Only grace can confront us in the right way. Only by first hearing that we are loved, madly and unconditionally, can we then hear the truth about us—including the ugly truths that we are not able to otherwise hear. In this chapter, we'll wrestle with a couple of meaty biblical texts about this ethics of butt-kickin' grace. But first, we'll have some fun with words, inspired by my twenty-five-year infatuation with the writings of Karl Barth.[1]

The Great *I* Behind the *I*

Get to know the great *I* behind the *I*, the Indicative behind the Imperative. It is square one of Christian ethics. Learn it and practice it every day, over and over again in the mirror.

---

1. Barth is the one theologian who always, *always*, makes me weep with joy over the God who loves in complete freedom. When I want that buzz, I mainline Karl Barth.

The Indicative

It all begins with mood. When we use verbs, we mostly use them in the indicative mood, which indicates something:

1. This banana is yellow.

2. The cat is on the mat.

3. Grover Cleveland was both the twenty-second and the twenty-fourth president of the United States of America.

Indicatives are matters of fact that relay some information to us.

The Imperative

However, not all verbs are stated in the indicative mood. There is also the imperative mood, which expresses a command or a request. Though it is not stated, the implied subject of imperative sentences is *you*.

1. Eat this banana!

2. Get that cat off of my precious antique mat I bought in Morocco!

3. Quit trying to impress me with your knowledge of the presidents!

Get it? The indicative indicates a state of affairs. The imperative is a command or a directive.

The Imperative Grounded in the Indicative

Now, what in Sam Hill does this little grammar lesson have to do with Christian ethics? Everything! In classic Reformation Christian ethics (the tradition of Augustine, Luther, Calvin, Kierkegaard, and Barth), the imperative of God's command is always grounded in the previous indicative of God's love. Yes, there is command, and it's as serious as a heart attack. But the imperative of the command is always *because of* the indicative of God's love that lies behind it all. And there you have it: the ethics of the great *I* behind the *I*, the indicative behind the imperative.

With this special secret gnosis in hand, let us now swap out our inane indicative and imperative examples and replace them with ones that are at the center of Christian proclamation. Ready?

> *Indicative:* God loves you like an only beloved child.
> *Imperative:* Live your life as a beloved child of God.

> *Indicative:* God first loved us.
> *Imperative:* We also ought to love one another.

> *Indicative:* Jesus loves you madly.
> *Imperative:* Love Jesus back.

> *Indicative:* Jesus Christ raises the dead.
> *Imperative:* Live your life as if you have nothing to lose.

This is the heart of Christian ethics. The indicative of God's love is always the basis for the imperative of God's command. Like Sonny and Cher, peanut butter and jelly, red wine and dark chocolate, they always go together.

For instance, let's see what happens if we take away either of these terms. What does Christian ethics become if we take away the imperative of God's command and simply have the indicative of God's love? Then we've got lots of love, but it doesn't go anywhere. God loves you, and that's about it. The First Church of the Indicative without the Imperative is all about the love. God loves you. It's Balloon Sunday all day, every day. Relax. Breathe. Have a cookie. Things aren't that bad. But there is no command, not even the command of grace. Here, God's grace doesn't manifest in anything we do. Grace doesn't take up residence here. It just sort of skims off the surface.

Conversely, what happens if we have only the imperative of God's command without the indicative of God's love that lies behind it? Then we have a cold, sheer, stark legalism. Ever been to the First Church of the Imperative without the Indicative? It's pretty scary. There are lots and lots of rules. You have to work really, really hard to make yourself right before God. And you live in constant fear that God will reject you. It is exhausting.

So remember square one, the great *I* behind the *I*. Behind the imperative of God's command is the indicative of God's love. God is sheer grace, but this grace is commanding grace. It seeks us out and wants to be made manifest in our lives.

The Yes and the Amen

Another way of putting this is found in the first chapter of 2 Corinthians, in the apostle Paul's musings about the great big radical yes of God's grace. Jesus loves you, right here and right now. Not the ideal you, but the you that you are. And not just you, but this whole bent and broken world. That is God's great big yes to us all. In Christ crucified, God speaks this great big strange and wonderful and shocking yes to the world. The message is not "Yes and no." It is all yes. In fact, even when we tried to say no, to kill this God, God threw it all back at us with the great big yes of the resurrection. And the spirit of this yes is alive, moving, groaning with creation in order to bring it to fulfillment. This yes is a bright light in the midst of our darkness—a light that shines even on the darkest nooks and crannies of our lives, in a way that heals and forgives and gets us unstuck with ourselves.

Paul makes it very clear that we are not the yes. We do not know how to say yes in this utterly grace-filled way. But we can say something else. We can say, "Amen." In other words, we can say, "Verily," "Let it be so," or "I second that emotion." Paul writes, "In Christ, every one of God's promises is a 'yes.' For this reason, it is through Christ that *we* say the 'amen,' to the glory of God" (2 Corinthians 1:20, NRSV). God says yes to us all. And we now have permission to say the amen—to create and build and grow, to be faithful to our friends and families and spouses. We have permission to be generous, to be forgiving; we have permission to change the world.

Election and Command

Call me a nerdy bookish, geeky academic if you must but, for my money, one of the most breathtakingly gorgeous books ever written is volume 2, part 2 of Karl Barth's epic *Church Dogmatics.* This work—"2.2" as we affectionately call it in the business—is divided into two parts. Yes indeed, this is volume two, part two, and it is divided into two parts. Part 1 is about election. Part 2 is about command.

Election, according to Barth, is "the sum of the gospel," the "best word we could ever hope to speak or to hear."[2] That God loves in freedom, commits Godself to this love, is the best word ever. God, in love, elects the other. God ordains that God should not be entirely self-sufficient, so God makes a self-election in favor of the other; God determines for Godself that overflowing, that movement, toward creatures and creation. In so doing, God elects an other as the object of God's love, and God draws this other toward Godself, so as never to be without the other. Since God is free, God elects the particular way in which God's love shall be shown: God elects the man of Nazareth, and through him, God elects God's people. Election is an election of grace and must be always be about God's love.

The command of this gracious God flows from this election of grace and, in fact, extends it, enfleshes it. Yes, God acts in God's free grace. But God also wills and expects and demands something of us, God's covenant partners. Encountering humanity in God's free love, God becomes the companion of us. The

2. Karl Barth, *Church Dogmatics,* vol. 2, *The Doctrine of God, Second Half-Volume* (Edinburgh: T. & T. Clark, 1957), 3.

love is unconditional, but so is the claim that God places upon us. This God who elects is also the God who commands. God is the judge, the one by whom we will be judged and also the one according to whom we must judge ourselves. God is the standard, the criterion, the question of good and evil, the rightness and wrongness of our activity. The elected one finds a Master and Lord. Grace does not will only to be received and known; it also wills to rule. It rules by offering us this Lord of the covenant. "There is no grace without the lordship and claim of grace."[3]

An Exercise: Reading Paul through the Lens of the *I* behind the *I*

The great indicative behind the imperative is all over the place in the writings of the apostle Paul. How can anyone possibly make sense of Paul's writings without seeing this? Take this little selection from Romans 6. It's easy to spot the imperative. Such is the command—serious as a heart attack. Allow me to paraphrase the imperatives, the commands, as found in Romans, chapter six:

- Let not sin reign in your body. (6:12)
- Do not yield your members to sin. (6:13)
- Yield yourselves to God. (6:13)
- Yield your members to God. (6:13)
- Yield your members to righteousness. (6:19)

If you look only at these imperatives, Paul will sound very stale and moralistic, like a bossy older sister, or a coach, or Mrs. Dornquast scolding you in Sunday school for stealing Todd Lundeen's paste and eating some of it.

But since you now know the great *I* behind the *I* (the indicative behind the imperative), you have already guessed that Paul is up to something way bigger and bolder and smarter and

---

3. Ibid., 12.

more revolutionary than simply giving a bunch of orders. Lying beneath these imperatives, giving them their source and life are the indicatives, the great big statements of grace (and again, I am paraphrasing):

- Sin will have no dominion over you. (6:14)
- You are not under law but under grace. (6:14)
- You were once slaves of sin; you have been set free from sin. (6:17-18)
- You are now slaves of righteousness. (6:18)

These are big, bold, beautiful statements. They are about grace. Grace is God's giving-ness—because that's who God is what God does. God is the giver. These big, bold statements are about God's unconditional love. It's like having someone come up to you and say to you, "You are loved. Beyond and apart from anything you say and do, you are loved." It's the ultimate affirmation. The old world has been cracked open, broken, undone. And what's opening up is this new space, the big space of grace.

Recall the error we often make when we are reading Paul: if you take the imperative (the command) without the indicative (God's love for you), then you get some sort of really tense moralism, which drives you away from Paul (and from the whole Christian thing in general). But you can also anticipate the big error that happens if you only take the indicative of God's love and pretend that there is no imperative of God's command. Then you end up with no ethic, no command, no recognition that something just might be wrong with the world, that people treat each other badly, that there is evil and injustice, and that this darkness just might run through your very own human heart.

When reading Paul, it is absolutely essential that we put the indicative and the imperative together. By doing so, we dive into Paul grace-first. We fling ourselves into this big space of grace. God loves us. That's why we are not supposed to hurt each other. God loves us. That's why we are supposed to share our resources and die to our self-obsession and let go of our lives that we might take them back again as a gift.

Newly tooled with the great *I* behind the *I*, let's look at how Paul uses some pretty standard Christian terms (sin, freedom, obedience) in some pretty daring and wonderful ways.

Sin

According to Paul, sin is not just "being naughty"; sin is not just breaking a rule. Sin is when we forget the big space of grace. For Paul, sin is no independent thing. It can only be understood against the space of grace. That's why, for Paul, even religion can be sinful, even religion can try to operate outside the space of grace.

Even the kind of sin that "reigns in our bodies" can be understood this way. "Let not sin therefore reign in your mortal body" (Romans 6:12, KJV), the text says. Isn't this something like our notion of addiction? Something that has a power over us, eats us up, and kills us, yet we deny that it is destructive? The way to overcome addiction is not through moral striving. The only way is to die. To hit bottom. To get baptized. To go under and come up again, knowing that we are alive, but also knowing how dead we really were.

Freedom

Paul is not a rugged-individualist American. Freedom, for Paul, doesn't mean the absence of all external constraints. In Paul's world, people were always connected; it was a question of whom or what you were connected to. For Paul, freedom means switching masters. "You have been set free from sin," means that you are now "slaves of righteousness" (Romans 6:18). At first blush, "slaves of righteousness" sounds downright scary. It sounds bad and boring and maybe even frightening. But read it this way:

"You are slaves; you are in service to righteousness, which is God's power to make things right." You are beholden, in service to, God's big grace. The grace of God has purchased you, and now you belong to God. Once you were free from righteousness; you were not connected to God's right-making-ness. But now you have been set free from sin and are in service to the righteousness of God, to God's big space of grace.[4]

Obedience

In Romans 6, Paul tells us, "Yield your members to righteousness" (v. 19). Now, in case you were wondering, "members" here does not mean your private parts. In Greek, this word stands for all your faculties and abilities and talents. And "righteousness" means the right-making capacity of God that we know in faith, the right-making-ness of God. For Paul, "Yield your members to righteousness," means, "Place yourself under God's grace," or, "All your faculties, talents, and gifts—give them all to the service of God's right-making-ness, God's grace." Obedience, for Paul, must be understood relationally. Through faith, we are in relationship with God, we trust in God; that's the basis of our obedience to the dos and don'ts.

---

4. You have been set free. God loves you unconditionally. You can do whatever you want, and God will still love you. God has to—because that's who God is and what God does. Is this really what Paul is saying? It doesn't make sense! Wouldn't that just make people want to sin more? This is not a new thought. Question 64 of the Heidelberg Catechism (sixteenth century) says, "But doth not this doctrine make for wild and careless folk?" (Karl Barth, vol. 4, pt. 1, *Church Dogmatics: The Doctrine of Reconciliation* [Edinburgh: T & T Clark, 1956], 642.)

Listen to the answer from the catechism: "No, for it is impossible that those who are implanted into Christ by true faith, should not bring forth the fruit of thanksgiving." (Ibid.) For those who have really understood and experienced grace, for those who have really had their boat rocked and their foundations shaken by that message of God's love, it is impossible for them to not be thankful and to "bring forth the fruit of thanksgiving" (to do good things and to do them in the right way).

Look at Jesus. (Paul is always looking at Jesus. He's down-right obsessed with Jesus.) These letters of Paul are letters written to real communities who were trying to live out the teachings of Jesus. Look at the Gospels, the stories of Jesus' life and teachings: Jesus is not a moralistic do-gooder. Jesus is passionate. He's a rebel. It's just that he is passionate about the right things, the things that matter. Jesus did not win a messiah badge for perfect attendance, for moral perfectionism. Jesus *trusted* God. They had a relationship of perfect trust. Jesus' obedience was a relational thing. That's the best model of obedience for us, too. We follow Jesus' call because we trust that it is the best thing for us—because, quite simply, God is *for us*.

That's what Paul tries to tell us in Romans 6:20-21. "When you were slaves of sin, you were free in regard to righteousness. So what advantage did you then get from the things of which you now are ashamed? The end of those things is death." Paul says: Hey, you used to be slaves of sin, but what return did you get? Was it really that great? But now that we know the truth, something else is grabbing hold of us. We might look back and long for the days when we were free from the knowledge of God's right-making-ness, but we can't go back. After all, do we really want to go back to business as usual? The only thing sin can pay us is death. How much better to follow Jesus in this big space of grace.

"Is It Possible to Love God?": A Bad Socratic Dialogue on the Subject of Christian Ethics

One serious contemporary Christian ethics question that we haven't really addressed yet is this: *It is possible to love God?* On the face of it, this seems to be the central question of Christian ethics. But it that even possible? To demonstrate what I mean, please allow me to close out this chapter on ethics with a rather grandiose *Bad Socratic Dialogue*. Hope this helps.

RELIGIOUS MAN *is our first character. He's a distinguished-looking professor type with thick graying hair. He wears a tweed jacket and smokes a pipe. He was educated in the '60s at a liberal East Coast seminary. He now hosts a radio show called* Speaking of Religion.

RELIGIOUS MAN. I love God. I love that moment of transcendence, when my spirit is lifted above the mundane. For I am Religious Man. And religion is not to be cast aside, in our rush to embrace the modern world. Religion is the exaltation of life, the intuition for the infinite of the universe. Though we may deny it, deep within all human experience are these religious impulses to love God and to love our neighbors as ourselves. To love is the greatest good. And to love God is the greatest of all loves. I love God. I am Religious Man.

LOVE SKEPTIC *is our next character. He's not nearly as refined as* RELIGIOUS MAN. *His favorite thing is to stay too late at the party and end up drawing you into a really intense argument. He used to be a minister, but something went wrong. We don't know what.*

LOVE SKEPTIC. I don't love God. I don't even know what that means. I don't *get* it. What does it mean to say, "I love God"? In fact, it sort of bugs me when people say they "love God." I'll tell you what I love: I love good food. I love traveling alone in a big, foreign city. I love stuff. And I love to buy stuff. I love sitting in my big chair with a little single-malt Scotch and getting sucked into a good novel while the snow is falling outside my window. I love my children and my wife (most of the time). I love my friends (usually).

RELIGIOUS MAN. I love those things as well—at least some of them. But I also love God. And I think I love God more than those other things. At least I *want* to love God more.

LOVE SKEPTIC. Aha! See. You *want* to love God more. But I don't think you do, and I don't think you can. So what's the point of obsessing about it? Do you really mean to tell me that you love God more than you love your best friend?

RELIGIOUS MAN. Well, I think I can—if I try.

LOVE SKEPTIC. You do, huh? Well, Religious Man, tell us. Please tell us your plan for loving God more.

RELIGIOUS MAN. Well, I believe I could pray more. Take up some form of meditation. Be more conscious of my surroundings. And just try to, perhaps, think about God more as I go about my day.

LOVE SKEPTIC. And you think those things will help you love God more? I still don't get it.

RELIGIOUS MAN. Well, don't you think we should try? Try to do our best to love God more every day? Isn't that important? Isn't that the most important thing in life?

LOVE SKEPTIC. What's the point? Besides, do you know how much damage has been done to the world in the name of trying to love God more? Do you know how much separation and violence that has caused? And you know what, Religious Man? I don't think you really love God. I think you love yourself, you big blowhard.

RELIGIOUS MAN. That's not very loving.

LOVE SKEPTIC. I'm sorry. It's just that, if you really think about it, so many forms of love turn out to be self-love. Take, for instance, your love for God: Aren't you just trying to project this image of yourself as connected to the divine? And you know what else bugs me? That religion stuff is so "modern," so "Enlightenment"—as if an isolated self can look within, discover the essence of "religion" or "spirituality," and then order his or her world according to it.

RELIGIOUS MAN. And I suppose you are "postmodern"?

LOVE SKEPTIC. I don't like that word. But yeah, I've read the stuff—those so called post-modern philosophers like Foucault and Derrida—and I think they make a lot of sense. I think religion has been one of the metanarratives we use to suppress and dominate otherness, difference, in the name of conformity and control.

RELIGIOUS MAN. That vocabulary seems a bit out of character for you. Perhaps your voice should be a little more consistent.

LOVE SKEPTIC. Hey, don't blame me. I didn't write this drivel.

At this point, we meet our third character. Her name is SOPHIA. *She's all of five feet tall, with dark hair and coal-black eyes. She's not a young woman, and you wouldn't call her cute. But there's something alluring about her.*

SOPHIA. Uh, hi, everyone. I couldn't help noticing that you two are stuck here. So I thought maybe I'd jump in and help out with this dead-end plot. My name is Sophia.

RELIGIOUS MAN. Where did *you* come from?

SOPHIA. Let's just say I've been around for a while.

LOVE SKEPTIC. Well, look who's come to rescue us. La-di-da. OK, Sophia, please. Save us.

SOPHIA. All right. Here's how I see things. You both make some very good points, but you've got no context, no history, no soul. You're out there in philosophical space, speculating. You are in your minds and not your bodies. You are not connecting with the stuff of the world. Forget about "love," in general. Let's all get smaller, more physical, and more particular.

Let's begin with Jesus' teaching in the Gospel of Mark. Jesus is asked, "Which commandment is the first of all?" And Jesus answers his own question: "The first is, 'Hear, O Israel, the Lord our God, the Lord is one; you shall love the Lord your God with all your heart, and with all your soul, and with

all your mind, and with all your strength.' The second is this,
'You shall love your neighbor as yourself.'"[5]

Now, my friends, it's so important to understand how
this text begins. Jesus begins with the Shema, the Hebrew
formula: "Hear O Israel, the Lord is our God, the Lord is
One." This throws us into our flesh and blood. It moves us
out of speculative, general philosophical space and places us
back in the world and in our bodies.

See, the commandment to love is not first given to
"humanity," to humankind in general. The commandment
is given to Israel, the people called and delivered and rescued by God. They were slaves in Egypt. God heard their
cries and delivered them, on account of Yahweh's *hesed*, God's
steadfast love. For no other reason than this: it is the nature
of this God to give, to rescue, to liberate! They are saved,
called, loved by God. They are called out, not to rule the
world, but to serve others.

So the commandment to love is grounded in God's first,
prior, preemptive love. And it's always that way in the Bible.
God's "love" is not an idea. Love is not speculative. Love is
a drama, a story. It is moving, going somewhere. This is not
love in general. This is love of a specific kind. This is not
"religious feeling" or a taste for the divine. This is about
being saved, liberated, rescued, freed from slavery by Yahweh, who is always opening up space that you thought was
closed.

RELIGIOUS MAN. What? Please tell us the meaning of "One Lord,"
as in "Hear O Israel, the Lord our God is One Lord"?

SOPHIA. It's about the uniqueness, the otherness, of Yahweh. This
Lord is different: One Lord, the only one who does what
this Lord does. Yahweh is the only steadfast lover. Yahweh

---

5. Mark 12:29-30.

intercedes for the people of Israel, gives it all away, suffers in their place.

LOVE SKEPTIC. It all sounds so controlling—to have a Lord who sits up in heaven and commands us. To me, it sounds pretty autocratic, hierarchical, even violent.

SOPHIA. This God doesn't control. This God lures the people into new spaces. This One Lord does not demand and claim and conquer. This One Lord is *good.* This One Lord gives and promises. And just because this One Lord gives away, there is no other command like this command. All other lords are something else. They want something else—our money, our soul, our mind, our body. But this Lord is different.

Unfortunately, humans are forgetful and hard of hearing. We forget that God has delivered us. Israel forgot that God had delivered them out of Egypt. They failed to be judged and ordered by steadfast love; they forgot to embody this love to the widow, the orphan, the stranger. And in the church, we forget also. We forget that God is our deliverer. We retreat from the world and set up this comfortable, cultural morality, instead of opening up that space for the other.

LOVE SKEPTIC. You're avoiding the question. The real issue is this: Jesus says "thou shalt." He commands us to love. How can we be commanded to love? How can love be demanded of us?

SOPHIA. Well, like I've been trying to tell you, the command to love is always rooted in God's prior and preemptive love. The good news of God's love is the only thing that *can* really command us, win us over, change us. Only love can make a real demand, the demand that really comes from God and really is received by us. And it is only in love that there can be real obedience, a real human answer to the divine love.

It's a bit of a paradox—as are the incarnation, the resurrection, and the mere fact of us. But it's a beautiful paradox; it is a "happy obligation." It's the yoke that is easy, the burden that is light. The command to love is not an alien demand that comes from an autocrat. It is given by one who has already deeply and intimately embraced us, one who has grabbed us and pulled us in, one who shows mercy, compassion, and kindness in the midst of hostility and violence.

"Christian ethics," if there is such a thing, is not about "loving God." It's about God loving us first. It's about letting yourself be loved. Even you!

LOVE SKEPTIC. What? After all this, it just turns out to be gooey personal piety? I mean, what you're sayin' is you've got this nice little tryst between you and God but the rest of the world can go to hell in a handbag.

SOPHIA. I'm not saying anything like that. In fact, I'm trying to show you how it's all about the *other*. Christian ethics is about relationship. We are chosen and loved, not in isolation. We are chosen and loved for the sake of others. Do you really want to imitate God, Religious Man? The way to imitate God is to love your neighbor as yourself. To embrace the other as God has embraced you. It's the only way I know that both respects the difference, the beauty, the otherness of the other and loves the other at the same time.

RELIGIOUS MAN. And who is my neighbor?

SOPHIA. Well, according to Jesus' answer to that question in Luke, your neighbor is the other, the different, the foreigner, the enemy—those your clan might consider beyond redemption. But again, let's stay concrete. The neighbor is not an idea. Neighbors are people, real flesh-and-blood people you live and work with every day.

LOVE SKEPTIC. But how can we love with all our heart, all our soul, all our mind, and all our strength? How can anyone possibly keep that up? I'm exhausted just thinking about it.

SOPHIA. You're right. It is impossible. I'd just add two things. First of all, try thinking of this love as being in a state of repentance. Think of the prodigal son, heading home to see his family again. You might say that he is, with his heart, soul, mind, and strength, in a "state of prodigality." He has turned his back on his isolation and he is headed home. He has heard the call. And this is his answer. He is heading for home. He wants to be back in relationship.

Second, you should know this, Love Skeptic. History is going somewhere. Yes, it takes time. But the Spirit of God's self-giving love, this Holy Spirit, she is at work in creation.

We live between the times—between the already and the not yet. But we look ahead to that day when our self-obsession and violence and rebellion are burned away and we *do* love God with all our heart, soul, mind, and strength.

RELIGIOUS MAN. Sophia, you've won me over. I hereby renounce religion forever. Long live relationship without religion.

LOVE SKEPTIC. You two make me ill.

RELIGIOUS MAN. I love you, Love Skeptic.

LOVE SKEPTIC. I refuse to be a part of this childish plot resolution. Someone's got to maintain some dignity around here.

RELIGIOUS MAN. I was thinking the same thing, actually. But we've got to come up with some kind of ending. Sophia? How do these Socratic dialogues usually end?

SOPHIA. I don't know. And I don't really like them, anyway. Too speculative. Ethics? Christian ethics ought to be more physical, more flesh and blood. Something we can see and hear and smell and touch and taste.

13

The Church: Everything You've Always Wanted to Know about Sects but Were Afraid to Ask

When your children ask you in time to come, "What is the meaning of the decrees and the statutes and the ordinances that the LORD our God has commanded you?" then you shall say to your children, "We were Pharaoh's slaves in Egypt, but the LORD brought us out of Egypt with a mighty hand. The LORD displayed before our eyes great and awesome signs and wonders against Egypt, against Pharaoh and all his household. He brought us out from there in order to bring us in, to give us the land that he promised on oath to our ancestors. Then the LORD commanded us to observe all these statutes, to fear the LORD our God, for our lasting good, so as to keep us alive, as is now the case."

—DEUTERONOMY 6:20-24

God's Forgetful People

I am not going to tell you everything there is to know about the church here. In countless books on historical theology, you can look up the history of the etymology of *ekklesia* (Greek for "gathering"), and you can look up the Constantinopolitan Supplement to the Nicene Creed (381), which attempted to set forth the four marks of the church: the church is "one, holy, catholic, and apostolic." But beware. There are generous readings of these attempts, and there are stingy ones.

But if there is a "people of God" through-line running through both testaments and played out in the history of the church, it is this: the people of God are a *forgetful* people. They are always forgetting what it's all about.

Take the church in our day, in our culture. Haven't we mostly forgotten that the church is not about condemnation but rather liberation? Haven't we forgotten that the church is not an end in itself but rather a means to the end of God's grace? Haven't we forgotten that the church is not the truth but rather a witness to the truth? Haven't we forgotten that the church is temporary and transient and is called to live its life for the sake of the world?

Theology is truly a gift here—theology that is humble and generous but nevertheless empowers us to do some important critical thinking about the church. Can we recognize ourselves in the Jesus story and still be critical of the church? We're trying to carve out that space here. It's something that I would call "critical Christian orthodoxy." Can we be critical of the history and tradition of the church? Can we own our share in the mistakes, the exclusions, and the downright violence in our church's history and still embrace the Jesus story? Critically orthodox Christians, unite! In Jesus Christ, God speaks a great big yes to the world, a yes that will outrun all the ways we try to say no. That's what we're trying to recover.

The Backstory: Liberation

You can't say they weren't warned, these people of Yahweh. They were warned, again and again, *not* to forget—not to forget who they were and where they came from.

In the little text from Deuteronomy at the beginning of this chapter, we get the story in a nutshell. Here's the setup: in the future, your children will have questions. They will ask why: "Why do we do this?" "What is the meaning of the decrees and statutes and the ordinances that the LORD our God has commanded you?" In other words, "Why all these rules?" and "Why this community?" and "Why should we worship and serve God?" and "What's the point?"

The all-important answer is *liberation*. That's it, pure and simple: liberation. When your children ask you in times to come, tell them the story: "We were Pharaoh's slaves in Egypt, but the LORD brought us out of Egypt with a mighty hand." It's the single most defining moment in the life of the Hebrew people. It's the claim that most clearly and boldly reveals their God, Yahweh. To this point, they really didn't know that much about this God. There were promises, there was forgiveness and covenant and renewal of covenant, but *this* is what defines the strange, mobile God of these ancient tribes. This God has a heart. This God has soul. This God hears their cries and delivers them.

"But We Want a King, like the Other Nations"

Countless believers have struggled mightily with the violence that leaps from the pages of the Hebrew Bible. And the worst part of the violence is no doubt the stories of the conquest of Canaan: blood, killing, entire cities eradicated—down to every last man, woman, and child.

Yet if you read these ancient texts with a bit of imagination mixed with a bit of help from the wisdom of our scholars, you begin to realize that the story of the conquest is not as tidy, as singular, as monolithic as it first appears. In fact, some of our best biblical scholars maintain that there is a lively and dynamic dialogue going on in these ancient documents.

The Hebrews were not like other nations. Instead of a king, they were ruled by a long succession of (more or less) wise judges. Judges handled disputes and provided leadership for the people. But the people grew unhappy with their judges. They wanted a king. They wanted more power, a stronger defense department, and more aggression against the enemies who attacked them.

In a key transitional passage from the Hebrew Bible, we have this argument between the last great judge, Samuel, and the Israelites. The people were tired of judges. They wanted a king, just like the other nations. Samuel warned them, the kings "will take" (1 Samuel 8:11, NRSV).

> He said, "These will be the ways of the king who will reign over you: he will take your sons and appoint them to his chariots and to be his horsemen, and to run before his chariots; and he will appoint for himself commanders of thousands and commanders of fifties, and some to plow his ground and to reap his harvest, and to make his implements of war and the equipment of his chariots. He will take your daughters to be perfumers and cooks and bakers. He will take the best of your fields and vineyards and olive orchards and give them to his courtiers. He will take one-tenth of your grain and of your vineyards and give it to his officers and his courtiers. He will take your male and female slaves, and the best of your cattle[b] and donkeys, and put them to his work. He will take one-tenth of your flocks, and you shall be his slaves. And in that day you will cry out because of your king, whom you have chosen for yourselves; but the Lord will not answer you in that day."

> But the people refused to listen to the voice of Samuel; they said, "No! We are determined to have a king over us,

so that we also may be like other nations, and that our king may govern us and go out before us and fight our battles." (1 Samuel 8:11-15, 18-20, NRSV)

The people didn't listen to Samuel. They really wanted a king.

And so the people entered into this period of kings. The kings were corrupt, aggressive, deceptive. And in almost every passage devoted to the kings leading the people into battle, there are signs that the whole thing was a mistake. As hard as that is to fathom at first blush, it doesn't take too much imagination to actually see these pro-king and anti-king factions carrying on a lively argument over the course of the conquest of Canaan as recorded in the book of Joshua.

Of course, this reading of the slow undoing of the violence projected onto God depends on a backward reading of the Bible. It's the prophets, centuries later, who most clearly and vividly and creatively tell the people all the things they forgot. The prophets tell them how they, the oppressed, turned into the oppressor. Meet the new boss, same as the old boss.

The prophets tell them that Yahweh is not bound to the land, that Yahweh wants Israel and Judah to *serve* and not to conquer, to be a light to the nations and not an empire. They are the chosen people, but they are chosen to be the suffering servant of Yahweh in the midst of rising and falling empires. The prophets proclaim that liberation is the *law*. The liberation of these slaves is supposed to expand and grow and be passed on to all of creation.

The Spirit Poured Out on the Church

Now let's jump way ahead to this second chapter of Acts, to the community of radical love—a kind of love commune that is centered around remembering the crucified and risen Christ:

They devoted themselves to the apostles' teaching and fellowship, to the breaking of bread and the prayers. Awe came upon everyone, because many wonders and signs were being done by the apostles. All who believed were together and had all things in common; they would sell their possessions and goods and distribute the proceeds to all, as any had need. Day by day, as they spent much time together in the temple, they broke bread at home and ate their food with glad and generous hearts, praising God and having the goodwill of all the people. And day by day the Lord added to their number those who were being saved. (Acts 2:42-47, NRSV)

Karl Marx, eat your heart out. It's a first-century version of a hippie commune. Sharing, giving, radical redistribution of wealth? No wonder "the Lord added to their number."

So why didn't it last? The love commune? Again, God's people are *forgetful*—forgetful of what it's all about. Just as in the Hebrew Bible, the history of Christendom plays out this same story. The oppressed become the oppressors. The church aligns itself with the empire. The love commune is seduced. The first four centuries of church history are the story of how the radical love commune becomes the great whore. Yes, the church itself became the great whore of Babylon, fornicating with the empire for the sake of power and status and wealth.

And it happens over and over again, throughout the church's history. From the crusades, to the corrupt popes, to the Third Reich and the "German Christian" movement and a church that did shockingly little to oppose the slaughter of six million Jews, to an Evangelical Christianity that stresses a personal relationship with Jesus at the expense of standing for justice and civil rights. We *are* a forgetful people.

Therefore, the church must not only be the place where we remember, it must also be the place where we remember how forgetful we are. The church must be a place where we *remember that we forget*.

But how do we remember in the right way? How do we be the church?

The Protestant Reformers stripped it all down to two key elements. Forget about all the institutional trappings, all the corruption, they claimed. The church is still the church (1) wherever the word is rightly proclaimed and (2) wherever the sacraments are properly administered.

First of all, proclaiming the word, in the right way, meant something very specific for them. It was the word of *grace*. It was not so much a literal reading of the Bible, but rather a liberating message that always, in some way, spoke the word that God is *for you*. They consciously owned their Christocentric reading of the Bible— that the four stories of Jesus were at the center. Thus, God's love revealed in the event of the death and resurrection of Christ became the hermeneutic, the lens, through which the Bible was read.

It *is* personal. The word frees us from our neat and tidy story of good reputation, of the facade of intelligence, goodness, and righteousness. We have this radical act of forgiveness. In this freedom, we no longer need to defend ourselves, for Jesus has already done this. The word strips us of our socially formed illusory selves so that we can join together in trust and love and unity and even attempt to do such things as that love commune in the second chapter of Acts.

All stripped down, the reformers pleaded their case. The Word of Christ is present among us whenever (1) the word is right proclaimed, and (2) the sacrament is properly administered. "The Word" means simply the word of God's grace that kills us and makes us alive again. "The Sacrament" is the visible, fleshy sign that this grace comes to us in our bodies, in our creation. In calling for the proper administration of the sacraments, the Reformers were referring first and foremost to the meal, the table, the Holy Eucharist. In the sacrament of Holy Communion, believers act out this spoken word of grace; they touch, taste, smell, chew, and swallow this grace that we cannot tell ourselves.

We all know it's not perfect. The church is forgetful. We can easily forget what it's all about. Let's admit it and own it can confess it right now. The church has a history of being seduced, of whoring itself to Babylon. Let's keep that in our frontal lobe.

But at its best, the church is a place of brokenness, woundedness, and vulnerability. The church is a place where we remember, we reorient, we dismantle the neat and tidy story we tell about our reputation. The church is a place where we are taken into and embraced by another story—the story of God's passionate and self-emptying love for us. The church forces us out of our dignity, our arrogance so we can jump into this beautiful but tangled web of relationship. The church is temporary and transient. At its best, in the image of Christ, the church is called to give its life for the sake of the world.

iiiiiiiiiiiii

A prayer for the church:

Gracious God, we give you thanks for your liberating love and for the freedom and creativity you bring to us in your word. We pray for the church, which bears the name of Christ. We confess its frailty, its futility, its outright rebellion against your grace. Transform your church, in all its crazy manifestations. Make your church a place of brokenness, vulnerability, and humility. Make us always aware of our forgetfulness. And empower us broken people to remember you in acts of kindness, encouragement, justice, and love. Amen.

Conclusion

So Much Straw: The Transience of Theology

Transient: passing especially quickly into and out of existence, passing through or by a place with only a brief stay or sojourn.

—*MERRIAM-WEBSTER ONLINE DICTIONARY*

THOMAS AQUINAS (1226–1274) WAS one of the great theologians of all time. His epic work *Summa Theologica* (The sum of theological knowledge) was nine years in the making and in current translations spans over thirty-five hundred pages. Yet three months before his death, Thomas received a revelation from God that summoned him to put down his pen and forever surrender his theological writing. "The end of all my labors has come," he confessed. "All that I have written appears to be as so much straw after the things that have been revealed to me."

So much straw? All those words, all those pages, all those countless hours? Really, Saint Thomas? Straw?

A few opponents of Thomas's tradition have interpreted
these words as a renunciation of his faith. But most historians
agree that this was something much different, and it brings us
to our point: the best theologians have a knack for reminding us
that theology is but a second-order discipline. It is always and
only dependent upon the encounter, the source, the real thing, the
address, the revelation of God. It is me, sitting in row 20 of the
737 before takeoff, struggling to explain to a Buddhist just why
my encounter with God through Jesus is so deeply meaningful.

Once again, I'll try to make this more clear:

- *The first order of God's revelation:* Christian faith is rooted
  in a first-order event of revelation: an *encounter* in which
  God is revealed through Scripture, preached word, sacrament, prayer, imagination, silent meditation, the created
  world, and other means. Christians display a wide variety
  of understandings as to *how* God is revealed, but they do
  believe in some sort of self-revelation of God as the source
  of their faith. Think of this first-order experience as the
  primary stuff of the divine encounter.[1]

- *The second-order task of theological reflection:* The practice of
  theological reflection, or "theology" for short, is the gift of
  stepping back from that first-order encounter and asking
  questions. If God speaks, how do we best understand? If
  there is a Word from God, what does it mean for humanity and for all of creation? How are we to behave? How do
  we be open to hearing that word again? How do we think
  critically about the ways in which this divine revelation
  has been distorted? And again, how has the church managed to turn the good news into bad—the bad news of
  shame, manipulation, and fear?

---

1. As I stated in my introduction, in classic Reformation-based Protestantism
(my tradition), this first-order event is called "proclamation," the preached word
of the love of God revealed in the life, teachings, and works of the risen and crucified Christ, interpreted and acted out in the sacrament of Holy Communion.

Do You Love Me?

Allow me to make this even clearer by leaning on an analogy penned by Gerhard Forde in the introduction to his classic *Theology Is for Proclamation*.[2] Forde asks the reader to picture a conversation between two lovers. They reach a critical moment in which the lover asks the beloved, "Do you love me?"

The beloved answers, "Well, that is an interesting question. What is love after all?" and so launches into a discussion about the essence of love. After patient waiting, the lover finally gets another chance. "Yes, that's all interesting, but do you love me?" Then the beloved takes another diversionary tack and says, "Well, yes, of course, I love everybody!" (A universalist!) The lover protests, "That's not what I mean! You haven't answered the question! Do *you* love *me*?" So it goes. In spite of all the helpful things it does, secondary discourse makes the would-be lover look ridiculous when it is substituted for primary discourse.[3]

For Forde, in the face of that ultimate question "Do you love me?" there is only one kind of discourse that will do the job. That is "primary discourse, the proclamation, the self-disclosure in present tense, first to second person address, the 'I love you,' and the subsequent confession, 'I love you too!' "[4]

Do you love me? It just might be the ultimate question of human existence. I've tried to make clear, throughout these chapters, that theology is not the source of this divine love. God's "I love you" to the world is the stuff of revelation, of address, of prayer and meditation and word and sacrament. Theology must always go back to its starting point: reflecting upon, contemplating, seeking to understand and clarify this encounter of God's unshakeable and sure "I love you" to the world. Thus, in the end, theology, too, ought to be about love, about the loving

---

2. Gerhard O. Forde, *Theology Is for Proclamation* (Minneapolis: Augsburg Fortress, 1990).
3. Ibid., 3.
4. Ibid.

relationship emptied out into all of creation in the life, death, and resurrection of Jesus, the risen victim who confronts us in our violence and shows us a new way to live. Theology must always defer to the first-order encounter with the living God.

Theology: Transient, Important, and Beautiful

Should you grow weary of all this reflection and analysis, this crazy history of old men fighting over doctrine, just repeat after me: "It's only theology; it's only theology; it's only theology." At their best, theologians own and even celebrate the transience of their craft. All theology is occasional, limited, disposable, contextual, and yes, transient. It's a second-order discipline that must always and forever be starting over again, dependent on a Word that lies outside of itself.

But this is not to deny the importance of theology. Claiming to receive a revelation from God is a very dangerous matter. And many have concluded that the outcome is not worth it. Why even mess with this divine revelation when history bears out the repeated theme of judgment, violence, and scapegoating our enemies and calling it "God's will"? Yet, for those who understand God's revelation as grace, as relational, as self-giving outpouring love for humans and for all of creation, this task of theology becomes a gift, a challenge, a passion.

Why mess with it? Because when someone who is skeptical but curious sits next to you on a plane, you might end up reflecting on your relational encounter with the living God all the way to San Francisco.

We need both: the first-order event of revelation and the second-order discipline of theology. And, in fact, all believers are theologians. We all put our trust in the divine encounter, that it is no delusion, that love is real, that it is revealed in flesh-and-blood relationships. Wherever your inquiries might take you, be you atheist, half-believer, or full-on washed-in-the-blood Christian, my wish is that you taste and see the transient, beautiful, crazy, mad gift of theology.

Are You a Christian?

"So you're a Christian?" I am a Christian only in the sense that in my best moments I know that I am claimed by Christ and named a beloved child of God. I need nothing. It's all been done. And I now have the freedom, the permission to love God back, to love the world, to engage and embrace all creatures and all of creation in the name of the self-emptying love of God.

"What does it mean to be a Christian?" The question stays with me. Perhaps it can't be put into words. Maybe the next time someone asks me that question, I'll whip out an easel and some oil paints and compose a hasty version of the holy mother and child or the bony finger of John the Baptist pointing to Jesus. Words so often fail.

So much straw. Yes, dear Thomas, that is the vision now, isn't it? I take back everything I just said. I hereby renounce it all. At least I hope to, one day. These are just words on a page: contextual, disposable, and transient. Like life. Here's hoping that we all might receive a revelation so clear and beautiful that all our words become as so much straw.

Afterword

Today, as I'm thinking about my friend Mark Stenberg and the book you've just read, I am reminded of our days at Bethel College, where Mark and I were roommates in 1979. The year 1979 was *the* time to get a Christian liberal-arts education, when it meant something. And by that I mean there was a lot of time to hang out and listen to music.

The year 1979 was also a great time to be listening to music. In the mid-'70s, we had just witnessed a major principality, the Top 40, lose ground to the plucky upstart, "album-oriented rock." And now "arena rock" was beginning to crash and burn as "punk rock" and "power pop" took off. The stage was being set for something amazing.

Mark and I met the first day of college, at a freshman mixer, and I liked him right away. Mostly, it was because he could quote Steve Martin's album *Let's Get Small* line for line. Also, like me, he appeared to feel really uncomfortable in a suit.

We met again a week later, by accident, at the Har Mar Mall (yes, the very place that soul singer Har Mar Superstar is named after). We ran into each other looking through the stacks of records at the Christian record store—both of us, separately, trying to make sense of it all.

We struck up a conversation: Given a choice, what music should we be spending our time listening to, Christian or secular? We felt obliged to listen to Christian albums. But to be honest, you couldn't compare them in quality; really, it wouldn't be fair (except for a few rare exceptions, like Bruce Cockburn and T-Bone Burnett, who weren't *really* considered Christian). It all felt a bit like eating your vegetables.

So we realized, as we looked through the record rack, that the Christian recording industry was out to counter this glaring gap in quality with some clever marketing. They were busy making these strange "smells like" albums to try to appease us, hoping no one would notice.

- There was a Christian version of Supertramp called Servant, and their album covers were pretty much indistinguishable.
- Dan Peek had migrated away from the pop trio America but had somehow found a way to make the same sugary pop songs to Jesus, rather than girls.
- And there was the Sweet Comfort Band, which we laughingly compared to a less hedonistic version of the Little River Band.

Yeah, Mark and I agreed, it was all feeling a bit candy ass. Something was missing. Who would bring the guts of the Jesus story to the masses through the all-important medium of the three-minute pop song?

Well, I'm happy to report that things finally fell into place when Bob Dylan went Christian that year with *Slow Train Coming*. This was profound; one of the most important voices of our time was "giving it to God!" Most of us church kids felt that it was all coming our way, and soon we'd be in on the ground floor of a massive social vanguard of *important* people coming to Christ! I mean, if Bob Dylan had "jumped the fence," who would be next? Neil Young? Led Zeppelin? The Clash?

Long story short, it didn't take. Bob Dylan moved on, or moved back, to being a great stylist, songwriter, and social critic who may or may not be talking about God within the lines of his songs.

That's the reason I love this guy Mark. He was the only one who got the irony of it all, right off the bat. We were getting caught up in the *campaign* of Christianity and losing the *relationship*. And that's what you've seen in this book. He understands the shame and manipulation and handcuffing morality of the faith we were handed—the "smells like" culture Christians are always trying to shill to each other. He knows those sort of tactics are only a temporary fix. But he also understands the grace, and his mission is to uncover and lift up the grace that was there all along.

We used to listen to music. Every day.

Joel Hodgson
Creator, *Mystery Science Theater 3000*